For my beloved Guru, Ralph Harris Houston

© 1971, Shizuye Takashima

Printing History

1971	First Canadian Printing
	Syndicated in eight major Canadian daily newspapers
1972	Second Canadian Printing
	'Best Illustrated Book of the Year' medal of
	Canadian Association of Children's Librarians
	'Look of Books' Design Award
1973	Third Canadian Printing
1974	First U.S. Edition, New York
	Japanese Edition, Fuzambo, Tokyo
	Sankei Shimbun Literary Award, Tokyo
1975	Musical Play by Gekidan Fuji, Tokyo
1976	First Canadian Paperback Printing
	Italian Edition PACCHI-DONO DAL GIAPPONE
	by Giunti Marzocco, Florence
	VI Premio Europeo di Letteratura Giovanile Award,
	Padova, Italy
1977	and every year thereafter
	A 'Choice' Book of the Children's Book Centre, Toronto
1979	Musical Play revival, Gekidan Fuji, Tokyo
1983	Second Canadian Paperback Printing
1988	Third Paperback Printing
1989	Fourth Paperback Printing
1991	Fifth Paperback Printing
	U.S. School and Library Edition, Children's Press, Chicago
1992	Sixth Paperback Printing

Canadian Cataloguing in Publication Data
Takashima, Shizuye
A child in prison camp

ISBN 0-88776-241-7

1. Takashima, Shizuye — Juvenile literature. 2. Japanese Canadians —
Evaluation and relocation, 1942-1945 — Personal narratives — Juvenile literature.
3. World War, 1939-1945 — Concentration camps — British Columbia — Juvenile
literature. I. Title.

D768.15.T34 1989 j940.54'72'71092 C89-090316-6

10 9 8 7 6
Published in Canada by Tundra Books of Montreal, Quebec H3G 1R4
and in the United States by Tundra Books of Northern New York,
Plattsburgh, NY 12901

Printed in Canada

A Child in Prison Camp

Takashima

Tundra Books

1

Vancouver, British Columbia
March 1942

Japan is at war with the United States, Great Britain and all
the Allied Countries, including Canada, the country of my
birth. My parents are Japanese, born in Japan, but they have
been Canadian citizens for many, many years, and have become
part of this young country. Now, overnight our rights as
Canadians are taken away. Mass evacuation for the Japanese!

"All the Japanese," it is carefully explained to me, "whether
we were born in Tokyo or in Vancouver are to be moved to
distant places. Away from the west coast of British Columbia
—for security reasons."

We must all leave, my sister Yuki, my older brother David, my
parents, our relatives—all.

The older men are the first to go. The government feels that
my father, or his friends, might sabotage the police and their
buildings. Imagine! I couldn't believe such stories, but
there is my father packing just his clothes in a small suitcase.

Yuki says, "They are going to the foothills of the Rockies, to
Tête Jaune. No one's there, and I guess they feel father won't
bomb the mountains."

The older people are very frightened. Mother is so upset; so are
all her friends. I, being only eleven, seem to be on the outside.

One March day, we go to the station to see father board the
train.

At the train station

An empty bottle is tossed in the air.
I stand away, hold my mother's hand.
Angry, dark curses, a scream. A train window is broken.

Most of the men have been drinking.
An angry man is shouting.
The men are dragged violently into the trains.
Father can be seen. He is being pushed onto the train.
He is on the steps, turns. His head is above the
shouting crowd. I see his mouth opening; he shouts
to his friends, waves his clenched fist.
But the words are lost in all the noise.
Mother holds my hand tightly.

A sharp police whistle blows.
My blood stops. We see a uniformed Mounted Police drag
an old man and hurl him into the train.
More curses, threats. The old train bellows
its starting sound. White, hellish smoke appears
from the top of its head. It grunts, gives another
shrill blast. Slowly, slowly, the engine comes to life.
I watch from where we stand, fascinated.
The huge, black, round, ugly wheels begin
to move slowly, then faster, and faster.
Finally, the engine, jet dark,
rears its body and moves with a lurch.
The remaining men rush toward the train,
scramble quickly into the moving machine.

Men crowd at the windows. Father is still on the steps,
he seems to be searching the crowd, finally sees us, waves.
Mother does not move. Yuki and I wave. Most remain still.
The dark, brown faces of the men become small.
Some are still shouting. Yuki moves closer to mother.

6

The long, narrow, old train quickly picks up speed
as it coils away along the tracks
away from all of us who are left at the station.

Mother is silent. I look at her.
I see tears are slowly falling. They remain
on her cheeks. I turn away, look around. The women
and the children stare at one another. Some women
cry right out loud. A bent old woman breaks out
into a Buddhist prayer, moves her orange beads
in her wrinkled hands, prays aloud to her God.
Mother and the other women bow their heads.
The silent God seems so far away.

Summer 1942

From March to September, 1942, my mother, my sister Yuki
and I are alone in Vancouver. David, our brother, is taken away,
for he is over eighteen and in good health. It's hard for me to
understand. Our David, who is so gentle, considered an enemy of
his own country. I wondered what he thought as his time
came to leave us. He spoke very little, but I do remember him
saying, "In a way it's better we leave. I am fired from my job.
The white people stare at me. The way things are, we'd starve
to death!"

Now our house is empty. What we can sell, we do for very
little money. Our radio, the police came and took away. Our
cousins who have acres of berry farm had to leave everything.
Trucks, tractors, land, it was all taken from them. They were
moved with only a few days notice to Vancouver.

Strange rumors are flying. We are not supposed to own anything! The government takes our home.

Mother does not know what to do now that father is not here and David too is taken. She does not speak very much; she is too worried how we are to eat with all her men gone. So finally, Yuki goes to work. She is sixteen; she becomes help for an elderly lady. She comes home once a week to be with us and seems so grown up.

I grow very close to my mother. Because we are alone, I often go to different places with her. Many Japanese families who were moved from the country towns such as Port Hammond and Steveston on the west coast of B.C., are now housed in the Exhibition grounds in Vancouver, waiting to be evacuated.

One very hot summer day mother and I visit a friend of hers who has been moved there.

A visit to the Exhibition grounds

The strong, summer July sun is over our heads
as we near the familiar Exhibition grounds.
But the scene is now quite different from the last time I saw it.
The music, the rollercoasters, the hawkers
with their bright balloons and sugar candy are not there.
Instead, tension and crying children greet us
as we approach the grounds. A strong odor hits us
as we enter: the unmistakable foul smell of cattle,
a mixture from their waste and sweat.
The animals were removed, but their stink remains.
It is very strong in the heat. I look at mother.
She exclaims, "We are treated like animals! "
I ask mother, "How can they sleep in such a stink? "
She looks at me. "Thank our Lord, we don't have to
live like them. So this is where they are.
They used to house the domestic animals here.
Such a karma! "

8

As we draw close to the concrete buildings, the stench
becomes so powerful in the hot, humid heat,
I want to turn and run. I gaze at my mother.
She only quickens her steps. It seems as if
we are visiting the hell-hole my Sunday school
teacher spoke of with such earnestness.

White, thin sheets are strung up
carelessly to block the view of prying eyes.
Steel bunkbeds, a few metal chairs, suitcases,
boxes, clothes hanging all over the place
to dry in the hot sour air, greet our eyes.
Mother sits on a chair, looks at her friend.
Mrs. Abe sits on the bed, nursing her baby.
The child, half asleep, noisily sucks her breast.
Mrs. Abe looks down at it, smiles,
looks at mother and says, "The food is much better now.
We complained every day, refused to eat one day.
They take all our belongings, even our husbands,
and house us like pigs, even try to feed us pigs' food! "

Mrs. Abe opens her heart to mother.
I look around. The children's voices
echo through the huge concrete buildings.
Some of them are running around. The cement floor
smells of strong chemical. I stare at
the gray, stained floor. Mrs. Abe seeing this, says
"They wash it every week with some cleaner.
As if they cared whether we lived or died."

A curious head pokes in from the drawn, frail curtain.
Mrs. Abe sees this, becomes angry, "Nosy bitch! "
she says aloud. The dark head disappears.
Mrs. Abe turns to me, glares into my eyes,
forgetting for a moment that I do not live here,
that I am still a child and am not responsible

for her unhappiness. I begin to feel uncomfortable.
I gently nudge my mother. She reads my sign,
rises to take her leave, bowing, speaking words of
encouragement. Mrs. Abe bows, thanks mother,
"You are lucky. You can still live in your house.
And your children are older. They are a comfort."
Her words trail off. She bursts into tears.
Her child awakens, startled; she begins to cry.
Several heads appear from behind the curtains,
eyes peer with curiosity. Mrs. Abe holds the child
close to her and weeps into its small neck.
I quietly walk away.

From the corner of my eye
I can see sweaty children; they gape at me.
They know I am from the outside. I pretend I do
not see them, I quicken my steps, I am outside.
Here the animal stench again overwhelms me.
I turn. Mother is behind me.
"You are rude to leave like that," she scolds.
Her dark eyes search mine. I feel bad,
I look down. The concrete ground seems to melt
from the blazing heat. I curl my toes in my
white, summer shoes. They are dusty from the walk.
I look up, "I'm sorry. I couldn't help it.
Her crying, and the smell...."
Mother takes my hand and we begin to walk
to the tram stop. "Someday, you'll understand.
Mrs. Abe is much younger than me. She is new
in this country, misses her family in Japan.
You know she has only her husband."

All the way home in the noisy tram, mother says
very little. I, happy to leave the smelly,
unhappy grounds, daydream. I think of the film with
Tyrone Power Yuki promised to take me to one day.

Vancouver
September 1942

Now we have curfew. All Japanese have to be indoors by ten P.M.
The war with Japan is fierce. People in the streets look at us with
anger. My sister Yuki has to quit her job. No reason is given
by the elderly lady. We wait, mother, Yuki and I, for our notice
to go to the camps. Already many families have left.

A night out

Yuki holds my hand, begins to run.
"We have to hurry, Shichan. It's close to ten.
Can you run a bit? "   "I'll try," I say,
but my limp makes it hard for me to keep up.
Yuki slows down. I wish mother were with us.
Everything seems so dark. An old man comes
towards us, peers at us in the dim light.
His small eyes narrow, he shouts, "Hey, you!
Get off our streets! " He waves his thin arms,
"I'll have the police after you."
Yuki pulls my arm, ignoring him, and we run faster
towards our house. The man screams after us.

Mother is at the door when we arrive.
She looks worried, "You are late." She sees us panting.
"Did you two have trouble? " She closes the door quickly.
"You know I worry when you're late, Yuki."
Yuki sits on a chair, looks at mother.
"I'm sorry. The film was longer than I thought.
It was so great we forgot about the curfew."

Mother pours Japanese green tea. It smells nice.
I sit beside her and drink the hot tea.
I look around. The rooms are bare.
Boxes are piled for storage in the small room upstairs.

Our suitcases are open, they are slowly being filled.
We are leaving for camp next week.

A siren screams in the night. Air-raid practice.
I go to the window. All our blinds are tightly drawn.
I peek out, carefully lifting them. I see
one by one the lights in the city vanish. Heavy
darkness and quiet covers Vancouver. It looks weird.
But the stars, high, high above, still sparkle,
not caring, still beautiful and happy. I feel sad
to be leaving the mountains, the lovely sea.
I have grown with them always near me.

"Come away from the window, Shichan." mother's voice
reaches me. I turn. I feel sadness come from her too.
She has lived here for so long:
"Over twenty-five years —hard to believe—
I was a young girl, full of dreams.
America! Canada! all sounded so magical in Japan.
Remember, we had no radio in those days, so all our
knowledge of this country came from books.
My own mother had come to Canada long before
other women. She was brave, not knowing the language,
young, adventurous, a widow with three children.
She took your uncle Fujiwara with her.
He was thirteen. I went to my grandmother's;
my sister, to an aunt. It seems so long ago."

Mother often talks of the past. Her life
on the tiny island sounds lovely, for she had
a happy childhood, so full of love.
I go to her. I see her hands folded neatly
on her lap. She always sits like this,
very quiet, calm. Her warm eyes behind her
round glasses are dark and not afraid.

An end to waiting

We have been waiting for months now. The Provincial
Government keeps changing the dates of our evacuation, first
from April, then from June, for different reasons: lack of
trains, the camps are not ready. We are given another final notice.
We dare not believe this is the one.

Mother is so anxious. She has just received a letter from father
that he is leaving his camp with others; the families will be
back together. I feel so happy. He writes that he is being
moved to a new camp, smaller than others, but it is supposed
to be located in one of the most beautiful spots in British
Columbia. It's near a small village, 1800 feet above sea level.
The Government wants the Japanese to build their own
sanatorium for the T.B. patients. I hear there are many Japanese
who have this disease, and the high altitude and dry air are
supposed to be good for them. I feel secretly happy for I
love the mountains. I shall miss the roaring sea, but we are to
be near a lake. Yuki says, "They decided all the male heads
of families are to rejoin their wives, but not the single men."
So, of course, David will remain in his camp, far away.

We rise early, very early, the morning we are to leave.
The city still sleeps. The fresh autumn air feels nice.
We have orders to be at the Exhibition grounds.
The train will leave from there, not from the station
where we said good-bye to father and to David.
We wait for the train in small groups scattered
alongside the track. There is no platform.
It is September 16. School has started. I think
of my school friends and wonder if I shall ever see
them again. The familiar mountains, all purple and
splendid, watch us from afar. The yellowy-orangy
sun slowly appears. We have been standing
for over an hour. The sun's warm rays reach us,

touch a child still sleeping in its
mother's arms, touch a tree, blades of grass.
All seems magical. I study the thin yellow rays
of the sun. I imagine a handsome prince will come and
carry us all away in a shining, gold carriage with
white horses. I daydream, and feel nice as long as I don't
think about leaving this city where I was born.

The crisp air becomes warmer. I shift my feet, restless.
Mother returns; she has been speaking to her friend,
"Everyone says we will have to wait for hours."
She bends, moves the bundles at our feet:
food, clothes for the journey. I am excited. This
is my first train ride! Yuki smiles, she too feels the
excitement of our journey. Several children cry,
weary of waiting. Their mothers' voices are heard, scolding.

Now the orange sun is far above our heads.
I hear the twelve o'clock whistle blow from a
nearby factory. Yuki asks me if I am tired.
I nod, "I don't feel tired yet, but I'm getting hungry."
We haven't eaten since six in the morning.
Names are being called over the loudspeaker.
One by one, families gather their belongings and
move towards the train. Finally, ours is called.
Yuki shouts, "That's us! " I shout, "Hooray! "
I take a small bag; Yuki and mother, the larger
ones and the suitcases. People stare as we walk
towards the train. It is some distance away.
I see the black, dull colored train. It looks
quite old. Somehow I had expected a shiny new one.
Yuki remarks, "I hope it moves. You never know
with the government." Mother looks, smiles,
"Never mind, as long as we get there. We aren't
going on a vacation; we are being evacuated."

Bang...bang...psst...the old train gurgles,
makes funny noises. I, seated by the window,
feel the wheels move, stop, move, stop.
Finally, I hear them begin to move in an
even rhythm slowly.

I look out the dusty window.
A number of people still wait their turn.
We wave. Children run after the train.
Gradually, it picks up speed. We pass the gray
granaries, tall and thin against the blue Vancouver sky.
The far mountains, tall pines, follow us
for a long time, until finally they are gone.

Mother sits opposite; she has her eyes closed,
her hands are on her lap. Yuki stares out the window.
A woman across the aisle quietly dabs her
tears with a white cloth. No one speaks.

2

New Denver, British Columbia
September 1942

After a day and a half on the train to Nelson, B.C., we ride on
an old bus for several hours. The bus climbs up, up, the steep,
narrow road hugging the mountains. I see the clear Kootenay
Lake from far above. It is lovely.

We are in a small village called New Denver, 700 miles
from Vancouver high in the Rocky Mountains.
Father is waiting with Mr. Fujiwara, our cousin,
at the small gas station. They both are brown from the sun and
seem to look different. I wonder if I too have changed in six
months. I feel suddenly shy as I peer at my father from the bus.

The tall, dark pine trees grow slender
along the round mountains that are so near.
We are in the wilderness. I hear the hammering
of the men as they build more houses.
It sounds friendly. More homes for the families.

Twice a week they arrive, from different parts
of British Columbia. Our cousins, the Fujiwaras,
are with us now. We are happy, for their children
have been our friends for many years and their
parents are close friends of ours.

Before me is our little new home.
It looks like a summer bungalow with shingle roof,
one square chimney in the middle, a door in the
center, two windows on either side of the
door. It still smells sharp from the wood.
I wrinkle my nose every time I go inside.

Everything is so new. All in a row, the same
houses are built; some are larger than others but all have the

same number of rooms, three; two bedrooms and
a kitchen in the center. The larger houses are for
families with many children. We, being only
four, have only one small bedroom and a kitchen
which we share with another family,
Mr. and Mrs. Kono. They have one child.

Our first walk to the nearby village

I walk with my sister Yuki. Around us are the
burnt trees. They sway gently in the soft
autumn wind. My sister takes my hand and guides me
through the narrow, fresh path to the main road.
The broken twigs and dry moss make crackling
sharp sounds under our feet. A fresh, lovely smell
of nature is about us.

We walk along the main road. This leads
to the tiny village of New Denver where our bus
from the train stopped. We look around.
There are no cars to be seen, even though the road is paved.

We see for the first time the office of the
Royal Canadian Mounted Police, half hidden among
the dark pines. Yuki looks, says, "You realize we are
no longer free to go from place to place." I stare at
the words, "R.C.M.P. Office" all in red. They seem
to grow larger before my eyes. Yuki continues,
"We even have to watch what we say or do." I look at
the closed door. Their power seems to come
through the very walls. We walk quietly past.

We see a Japanese man, much like our father,
walking along the highway: he is walking towards us.

He is carrying a short stick and has a band around his
arm. I wonder who he is. I stare. The slender, thin man
smiles slowly at us; his tiny, black moustache looks unreal.
Yuki nudges me: "He's one of the World War I veterans
who are hired by the R.C.M.P. to watch over us. Dad says
there's quite a number of them here." I feel really bad now.

"Do they always carry a stick?" "Yes," replies Yuki,
"but you know, Shichan, it may sound nuts to you,
but he's no more free than we are. He must report to
the Police if anything is wrong or anyone does anything
suspicious. We are not free, but neither is he."

I feel confused and mad. I want to shout and protest
but I remain silent and hold my sister's hand tightly.

As we walk away, the beautiful,
silent nature surrounds us, quietening.
The office of the Police fades, is replaced by the
sight of a small river. We cross the narrow steel
bridge and I see the river roaring with great strength.
Finally, past the bridge, across an apple orchard,
the village is reached. It has only a few stores,
no traffic lights, or buses and streetcars;
so different from the Vancouver we have left,
was it only a few days ago?

New Denver is a toy-town,
resting gently in the middle of all these mountains.
Two grocery stores, a butcher shop,
a hardware store, a drugstore, the rest are houses,
all neat in a row, not new, not old, just houses
of wood with neat picket fences and kept gardens.

Yuki and I see some villagers. They stare. We do
not speak. Later, I learn they were amazed we could

speak English so well, and even wore shoes.

We buy what we need, even if the prices are high.
The cost of food has soared. We were warned
the villagers are trying to take advantage of us. I see
Yuki is furious. She tells one old grocery man that
he's a thief for charging fifty cents for a head of celery...
the old man wipes his mouth; his blue eyes narrow,
squint and stare. He shrugs his shoulders and says,
"This is wartime. Everything is expensive."
"Yes," replies Yuki, "especially for us."

We shop quickly. The meat store keepers are the same.
They charge us a lot of money for a roast.
Yuki has another fight. One thing, she always speaks up.
On the way home, Yuki decides to try another route.
She says angrily, "I don't feel like bumping into
these people who rob us."

We come to a small park. There is no one here.
From the edge of this park we look down.
The view is lovely. Slocan Lake is in full view.
The green, clear water reflects the blue sky,
the mountains. We sit. All is still.

The lush grass feels soft, damp. A friendly tree is
near us. I look at Yuki. She gives me some candies,
jelly beans, two black ones, my favorite.
Surprised and happy I place one carefully in my mouth.
The round, sweet candy melts slowly; its
licorice flavor oozes out. I close my eyes in wonder.
After the sweet taste is gone I open my eyes.
It's close to noon. The fall sun is above us.
The overhead sky is blue, blue.

Yuki is looking at the lake, the distant trees.
I ask, "Are you happy here, Yuki?"
She is silent. I wonder if she's going to cry.
Her face turns to mine; she smiles.
Her dark-brown, tilted eyes are warm.

Quietly, she takes my hand,
speaks, "I try to be. We must try not to
be sad or angry. It would not help things. Mother...."
Her voice trails off. I understand. I nod.

To break the mood I stick out my tongue to show how
black it's become. Yuki shows hers. It is black, too.
We laugh. She gives me several more jelly beans.
"For later, after lunch" she warns. But they
look so lovely and almost sparkly in my moist
anxious hand. The red color stains my palm.
I look at my sister. As always she reads my thoughts.
"Put them in your pocket," she commands. I obey
with regret, making a face of anguish.

We go on home slowly. The multi-colored candies
rattle merrily in my blue jacket pocket.

Our home at night

It is night. We light our two candles.
There is no electricity.
The frail, rationed candles burst into life and
the darkness slinks away. The smell of fresh-cut trees
burning, fills the room. The pine pitch cracks and pops
in the fire. I sit, watch my mother.
She places the rice pot on the black, heavy stove.
The wet, shiny pot begins to sputter.

"Rice tastes better cooked like this," she says,
smiles. Her dark eyes look even darker in this semi-light
and I feel love for her. "Why? " I ask. "Because natural
fire is best for cooking. Food tastes pure."
I stare at the now boiling rice and wonder why all people
do not use such stoves and fuel.

Yuki brings wood. I help her pile it near the
hot stove, for the raw wood is damp.
The family who share the kitchen, the stove and
the house, begin their dinner. Mrs. Kono appears
quietly from her nooklike curtained bedroom,
bows to my mother, washes her rice. The wood sink
gurgles as the water scooped from the lake
plunges quickly down the narrow pipe.
Soon her rice too is cooking on the big,
black stove. The bare, tiny, candle-lit room is
filled with the smell of rice and Japanese food.
Mrs. Kono is still young. I notice she watches her
rice pot with care as mother does. "This is very important,"
mother has often said.

Mrs. Kono lives with her husband and their small child,
a girl of three. Kay-ko is her name.
A lovely girl with black, black hair cut in
straight bangs, huge round dark eyes that look
very merry when she smiles. She always has
rosy, rosy cheeks. Now she comes shyly to me,
calls me "Big Sister" in Japanese, which sounds
nice, for I have never been called this.
I smile. She squats and watches as I pile the wood.
The white part of the wood looks strange in
this dim light. "Would you like to help? " I ask.
Half joking, she nods, begins to hand me the pieces,
one by one with her tiny, round hands. Some of the
pitch sticks to our hands. I look at the sticky, yellow

liquid coming out of the wood. Kay-ko stares at it.
"What is it? It smells funny." I reply, "It's pitch. Comes
from the pine tree. We learnt this in school."
Yuki joins in and adds, "It's the sap of the tree.
It's full of the sun's energy. This is why it
cracks and pops as it burns." Kay-ko and I both
listen, and we hear the sharp snap of the pitch
burning. The fresh smell of the pine reaches us.
We both wrinkle our noses. Kay-ko laughs.
I dab a bit of soft pitch on her nose; she does
the same to me. Soon we forget all about piling
the wood and end up laughing and laughing.

The table is set; the white candles create a circle
of light on the wood table. I sit by the flame.
I notice the far corners of the room are dark. This
gives an eerie feeling. Though eyes and mind are getting
used to this kind of light. On the other
side of the room I can hear the Konos talking quietly.
It took us several days to get used to living with them.
But the Konos are so quiet, speak very little,
except for Kay-ko, who talks a lot. I do not mind.
I think it bothers my mother and father more.
Older people seem more sensitive to other people's noises.
I'm glad I'm still young, for things do
not bother me, even as much as they bother Yuki.

I hear Mr. Kono talking to my father. "It's a
blessing our children are healthy and do not mind this.
Imagine eating by candlelight. No water."
Father replies, "We're complaining to the B.C. Security
Commission again. We won't give in. We cannot walk a mile
for drinking water, with the winter coming." Mr. Kono asks,
"Will they listen? " Father's voice is impatient:
"They will have to. After all, it's beyond human dignity."

22

A strike is called

Tonight father returns home angry.
He tells us this story: "The men who are disabled
or too old to work have been getting twenty-three
dollars a month from the Provincial Government.
They were told from now on they
must pay eleven dollars monthly rent
for their shacks. And yet another outrage.
The Police have closed the houses where the elderly
bachelors and widowers live and locked the doors.
They even took all their food away. Some of
their friends have taken them in.
We've had enough! We are all furious."

Even I am surprised. Goodness, what next?
Father sits silent now. There is a terrible tension
in the air. Suddenly, father stands up, shouts,
"We do not work tomorrow." I jump.
Mother nudges me, a sign to remain silent.
Yuki goes out of the house. I look at mother.
"What do you mean? " she asks.
"We'll go on strike," father announces.
He rises, goes out of the house.
The door slams. Kay-ko starts to cry.
Mrs. Kono gasps. "My," she says, dropping
her chopsticks on the table. Mother utters a curse,
then apologizes to the Konos.
Mr. Kono looks at us, says with fury, "Imagine,
treating the old men like that. When the high
rent was ordered, the men complained.
They were already having such a bad time
fetching drinking water from such a great
distance. The Police closed their homes and
took their food away. I don't blame your husband
for being so angry." Our supper is forgotten.

A quarrel

We hear noise outside. We all go out, the Konos,
mother and I. I see all our neighbors are out too.
The terrible news has reached everyone's ears.
Mr. Nishimura across the street is shouting at his wife.
She is shouting something to him, her mouth
gaping and hollow. Mr. Fujiwara, our cousin, is there,
talking, for they live close to us. I look
around for Yuki. I see her in the distance with Rose.

Everywhere people are shouting. At the center
is Mr. Mori, an old, brown-faced man with
sunken cheeks. Like the moustached man
on the highway, he is hired to "keep an eye on"
his people. No one likes him or trusts him.
He seems to belong to the outside and is
not one of us. Probably, he feels this.
Maybe he doesn't like having to work for the
Police, so he turns his anger towards father
and his own people. Suddenly everyone is silent,
staring at him. He glares back, then waves
his stick before father's face, shouts again,
"If I were younger, I'd do something about our situation.
You are all cowards. I fought for Canada
in the Great War. I am a war veteran, not a dog
as you whisper behind my back. This is my job."
Father stares at Mr. Mori and shouts,
"Shut up, old fool. Working for the Police
is the same as spying for them. Leave us alone.
This is not your business. We do not need your advice.
Lot of good it's done you being a veteran. You can't vote
any more than we can. British Columbia won't let orientals
vote—veteran, citizen, or police-spy."

The old man stares, seems to shrink smaller.

He curses violently, and spits at my father's feet.
Father glares, grabs him by the collar.
I get scared then. I start to cry.
Mrs. Kono screams. Mother takes my arm.
Hell breaks loose. "I'll have the R.C.M.P. after you! "
shouts the old man, as he is dragged away from father.
Someone cries, "Trouble maker! " to my father and
to the other men. Women are shouting and crying.
Mother pushes me back into the house. Through
the thin walls shouts can still be heard.
Mother looks at me. "Don't cry. Everything
will be alright." She sits by the table. "Try to eat."
Quietly, I pick up my orange chopsticks
and begin to eat. The rice is cold.

Yuki does not come home for a long time.
She often goes to Rose's when things
become unbearable at home. Being older, she finds
things harder, I guess. She doesn't tell me how she feels.
She thinks I'm still a baby and wouldn't understand.

Later mother says, "If it wasn't for the few like
your father who complained to the Government,
we would not even have stoves to cook with."
I nod. The house is still now. At last Yuki returns.
She does not speak; she goes to bed.
Mother ignores her. I too creep into bed.
I touch my sister's feet. She draws away and turns
her head. I can hear someone crying. It's muffled.
I remain still. I hear the wild dogs howl. The owls
screech in the wilderness. They add to the awful feeling
in our house. I long to be with the owls, the wild animals,
away from all this. I wish I were older, then
I could go away. At last, slowly, sleep overtakes me
and I soar into another happier world.

3

School
October 1942

The strike does not last long. "There is no unity in our community. Always selfish people, wanting their own gain and this terrible fear." I hear father speaking to mother. So he and others who had complained return to work within a few days. Rent is charged to the elderly and the disabled. The bachelors' house is finally re-opened. We continue to live with the Konos.

One afternoon the Police come to our house. A big, tall, blond man asks my father many questions. Father does not give any names, and quietly says he is not afraid. The Police leave. Mother is very upset. Father says someone must have reported him to the R.C.M.P. You can't trust anyone. He is angry. Nothing happens after the visit, but I think father is often looked at with suspicion, for he is so outspoken and sharp.

Meanwhile school for us has not begun. I am getting restless. The Provincial Government of B.C. claims that the Japanese people do not deserve an education. Yet, father says, they are taking tax money for education as well as rent for our houses. Can you imagine? Every day the elders bravely complain to the B.C. Security Commission. Finally, during the last week of October, school starts for the children, but just from grades one to eight. "The Japanese people do not need, nor do they deserve, higher education." Father says that's what they told him and Mr. Sumi, our other spokesman. So Yuki cannot finish high school and she has only one more year to go. Mother is very upset. Yuki remains quiet.

We are taught by older girls. They have completed high school, but they are not "teachers," so everything is noisy and very un-school-like at first. We are given correspondence sheets which we must follow. I don't like this at all. We have books, too, but nothing else. I miss the familiar desks and my school friends.

First days of school

I stare at the boy sitting beside me.
Feeling my eyes, he turns, smiles gently.
I feel warmth towards him. I wonder what his name is.
Too shy to ask, I return my gaze to our teacher.

End of October. I feel the cold
of the winter wind. It seeps through the paper-thin
walls of the houses. The class is held in a
house the same as ours, only there is one big
room, not three. Each class or grade has one house.
I hear the wind outside. Our black, pot-fat
stove is in the far corner of the room. I cannot
feel the heat. I bend forward and put my hands in
my overcoat. I wish I were home. I sigh.

"Will you stand up." Startled, I look up.
Miss Mizuno, our teacher, is staring at me.
I obey. "Now," Miss Mizuno continues, "can you
tell us your name, where you lived before coming
to New Denver? " I stare out the window. I feel like
saying "Marco Polo's daughter and I just came
from China, with camels, bells and all,"
for I had just been reading about it.
I can almost see the brown, funny-looking
camels with the fur-capped Tartars. I start to
smile, forgetting all about Miss Mizuno, her
question, the class room. I look down at the wooden
desk, turn to the boy next to me. Miss Mizuno's
voice reaches me from far away. The other students
snicker. The boy next to me whispers, "Your name? "
"Oh, yes, I forgot! " meaning the question, not my
name. Everybody starts to laugh, the boy
next to me the loudest. Miss Mizuno is angry.

"Go outside until you can behave and
remember your name." Miss Mizuno turns
all red, opens the door. I hurry out,
for I have started to laugh, too, and once I start,
I know I will not stop. The door slams after me.
I can still hear laughter. "Class behave! "
the teacher commands. I sit on the steps outside the school
trying not to laugh. Then I hear the door open
once more. I turn. It is the boy who shares my desk.
The door slams behind him, too. Silence.
He sits beside me on the narrow steps, he smiles,
squints his dark eyes. "Teachers are funny people.
What were you daydreaming about? "
I tell him, "Marco Polo. Can you imagine
if I came down the streets with all
my camels and servants, with jewels and bells.
It's so lovely. I wish I could travel. It's so dull.
These dumb schools. I know how to read now
and write. I don't see why I have to learn
all the other things." The boy stands up
and walks away. I follow. "Do you think
you'll travel when you're older? " he asks.
"Yes, I promise myself every night before
I go to sleep that I will go far, far away, and
see all the lovely countries. Don't you want to
travel? " The boy stares into my eyes; his reflect
the dull fall sun, seem so full of dreams.
"Yes. But, you know, my mother is not well."

I stand up, look away, feel sad. I look at the gray,
pale sky. The smoke from the schoolhouse
chimneys curls up, up, into the wide, empty sky.
I feel the cold wind against my face.
The boy stands too and stares at the sky.

Our first snow

We children continue to go to school. It was not the best, but
school is school and I have no choice. Finally, our first sign of
winter.

As I pick my way along the brushes, stumps
and broken, twisted twigs and grass
(a short cut from the school to our home)
I see our first snow. It falls quietly,
gently from the low, gray cloud.
I stop, put out my hands. The star pattern of
the snow looks perfect as it falls on my hand.
I wonder how it can be so lovely.
I touch it carefully with my other hand.
But then, as if I have broken its secret,
it melts, leaving a tiny, clear drop of water.
I try it again. The same thing happens. I look up.
Now it's beginning to snow harder. I hurry home.
The tall grass and dead leaves feel wet.
I'm excited and happy.

That night Yuki and I stare out of our small window.
The snow has stopped. We see the lemony-yellow
moon shine so nice and bright, her silver falling
on the white earth. It looks beautiful.
The trees outside are heavy with snow.
Their dark green, spiky branches are hidden.
The shimmering, winter magic light makes
the neighbors' houses look suddenly beautiful.
How kind snow is!

"Yuki, is your friend Rose coming? "
Yuki replies, "Yes, she should be here soon.
I'm making some hot chocolate, and
mother bought a cake." I wonder if I

can stay up too. I wish I were older.
It seems unfair to have to go to bed so early.
I finally ask, "Can I stay up for awhile?
Please. Mom is out. She won't know.
And dad's gone to play cards." Yuki stares
out the window. "There she is. Rose." I peek out.
Then I see her walking slowly towards our house.
Her tall, thin body is bent forward. The snow is
all around her, all white and magic. "Okay, Shichan.
You can have hot chocolate and a piece of cake.
Maybe we could have it now. It's cold. Then you
can go to bed before mother comes home. Alright? "
I feel so happy. I rush to the shelves to bring
out the cups. Yuki goes to the door to let Rose in.
The cold air comes rushing from the open door.
I put out the big pot for the hot chocolate.
The big, black stove is hot and warm. I
smile at Rose. She is bundled up like a hunter.
"Hi! Yuki's making hot chocolate." Rose nods,
too cold to speak. I laugh. We all laugh.

The small candle casts an orange glow on my book.
I am reading about Marco Polo again.
My mind leaves our house. I hear Yuki and Rose
talking quietly, but soon their voices fade away.
I feel like a princess being rescued by a brave,
dark Tartar. I see the Chinese palace as my hero
carries me to his emperor's magnificent summer home,
all tiled and mosaic, filled with fountains
in the lush gardens. I close my eyes, and dream.
The Tartar comes to life, hands me splendid jewels
to be placed around my hair. He takes my hand
and guides me gently into the garden.
I am not afraid as I reach for another world.

4

Winter 1942

We must walk over a mile into the village for our drinking water.
The water from the lake is not pure, and we are told not to drink
it, even if it is boiled. There is an old mine up in the mountains,
not far from New Denver. It is closed now, but during the time it
was open, the miners threw all their waste into the stream which
gushes down the mountains into Lake Slocan. It's the same small
river we cross going into the village. So even if this lake looks
lovely and pure, the water is not to be drunk. We may use it
only to do our dishes and wash our clothes. Almost everyday, we
go to fetch drinking water. Yuki goes most of the time now that
I am at school.

Today is Saturday. We hear that the Spanish delegate and the Red
Cross people are touring the camps because of so many complaints
by our parents. Everybody is excited. "Maybe we'll have water in
our homes," I tell mother. She smiles and hands me the kettle.

A visit from the Red Cross

Yuki and I walk with care along the path.
The snow-covered ground feels soft under our feet.
I carry a kettle full of water; Yuki, two buckets.

In the distance I see the Red Cross people and another
man, all in smart winter overcoats with briefcases.
They stop to watch us with our buckets of water.
We walk past them. The sharp-faced man with glasses
and dark, wavy hair, very Spanish, stares at us, turns
to his companion and says: "And they have no light?"

The old, dark Japanese man, the veteran who had shouted
at father, comes towards the small group of men.

He says aloud in English, "And we have to read and work
with candles, and they're rationed. Our eyes are ruined."
He waves his cane. I find it odd. He was angry with father
when father criticized, and now he is saying the
same things. I thought he was on their side;
but he sounds as if he's taking our part. The delegates
stare at him. The R.C.M.P. men move closer; they look
embarrassed and shrug their shoulders. Mr. Sumi
is standing and talking with father. He pulls
the old man away. "We are doing what we can.
Go home and wait." The old man's eyes turn
wild again. He spits on the snow. Yuki calls,
"Come on, we have to go. Mom's waiting for the water."
So I hurry after her. I hear shouts in the distance
but do not turn. I see the beautiful snow-capped
mountains across the still, winter lake.
They seem so still, so uncaring, so unchanged.
Slowly, they overcome my other unpleasant
thoughts, and peace is with me again.
"Isn't it lovely? " I ask Yuki. "Yes. Better not
to see the fight if there is going to be one. We
can't do anything." Down below, the birds fly
close to the lake, skimming it with their wings.
They look so happy, the birds....

Several days later, father brings home a lamp.
So does Mr. Kono. One coal-oil lamp
has been given to each family by the Security
Commission. It is hard to believe. Father has a
triumphant smile on his face as he carries it in.
He places it gently on our table, "Well, this
will give us better light to cook and read."
Seeing me staring, he adds: "Since you do most
of the cooking, Shichan." I laugh and look at
the new lamp. Its metal parts shine, the round
glass part looks lovely. I touch it with my hands.

Mother comes closer, smiles. She too looks happy.

That night the lamp glows merrily on our dinner table.
The sharp smell of oil is pleasant. I look across
the room. Mrs. Kono's lamp is glowing on her table
too. Kay-ko is staring at it. She turns, smiles and
presses her eyes together. "I have one too! "
she shouts from her seat. Her father says,
"They're eating. You mustn't shout." I only nod.
Father says, "One step at a time. Next comes
water... in the spring."

Our first Christmas
1942

Finally, finally, it is Christmas! A Christmas so different from all
the others of my life. We have snow the day before. In the evening
father starts preparations for our Christmas dinner.

I awake, I feel strange. Then I remember.
It is Christmas. I move my legs, then my arms.
They awake slowly from their sleep. I open my arms.
I feel for Yuki. She is not there. I sit up with a start.
I feel the cold air. It is so very cold. Our stove
must have gone out! I crawl back into bed,
I try to move my pillow. It is stuck again
to the damp, cold walls.

"Shichan, wake up." It is Yuki. She nudges my feet.
Then I remember I had told her I'd get up early
and go to Communion with her. The seven-thirty service.
I slowly re-open my eyes. It is still dark. I crawl out of
our bunkbed. Everyone is still asleep.

We step outside. The snow is fresh, but not too deep.
The early morning light is gently beginning to show.
Quietly, we begin to walk through the silent,
white world around us. We do not speak
for a long time. After a while I turn.
I see our footprints on the fresh, powderlike snow.
I squeeze my sister's hand. I smile at her. I feel
the happiness in her, too. Then, I remember,
"yuki" means "snow" in Japanese.
"Why did mother name you Yuki? " "I don't know.
She said she was so happy when I was born.
Maybe I reminded her of something nice
in her happiness." "It's a nice name."
Yuki nods, points to our footprints. "See, we're the
first ones to walk on this road today." We turn
our heads toward the snow-covered mountains.
Way below from the bridge, we can see the gray water
of the river, swollen and angry as it rushes away
around the bend with a great, loud roar.

The church bells ring in the distance, clear and
distinct, telling us to hasten. The mountains,
the snow-covered firs and pine trees listen. We turn
and hurry towards the sound of the silvery bells.
All seems like a dream, the snow, the bells, our
silent steps on the white winter carpet. As we hurry,
I think of our Lord, being born this day, in a
strange land, on such a winter as this.

"Do you think it was as cold, that winter when Jesus
was born? " I ask Yuki. She looks at me.
Her face looks serious, "Really, I don't know.
You ask the funniest things."

The church is tiny, half hidden by tall pine trees.
There is a small sign on the snow-covered lawn:

"Christmas Communion — 7:30 A.M.
St. Paul's Anglican Church." We enter.
It is dimly lit. The tall, narrow candles
cast a lovely glow on the altar. I stare at them
fascinated. There are holly leaves and flowers
on the altar with the Cross. Everything has a
magic look. I feel close and happy to be here.
I look at Yuki. Her eyes are closed.
I close mine and pray.

As we leave, a few people in the church nod
and wish us "Merry Christmas." Many do not,
for they are not supposed to be too friendly
towards us. But I'm used to it now, or like to
think I am. Our new minister, a young man
in his twenties, is at the door. He is shaking hands
with everyone, whispering holiday cheers
and blessings. As our turn approaches,
I wonder if he will be pleasant. He may pretend
not to like us because of the people around him.
I feel very uncomfortable. Yuki stares ahead,
walks toward the minister. I follow.
Our turn comes. He holds out his hand.
His clear, pale blue eyes behind his gold-rimmed
glasses are friendly. His warm feeling comes
towards us. "Merry Christmas, Yuki.
And Shichan, my blessings and the Lord's.
How are your parents, your mother? "
He says this aloud. "Fine, thank you. Merry Christmas."
We both say this with happiness.

I like the new minister. Reverend Hailly
is very nice, not cold like the other one
that left soon after we arrived in New Denver.
He came to see mother the other day and
greeted her in Japanese. He told her he is

studying the Japanese language.
Mother was delighted. So this day, on our
way home, our feet seem lighter. The day is on
its way. The early sunlight glows on the white
pure world. The winter birds are singing.
All is splendid and lovely....

Christmas at home

I swing my legs to and fro. Japanese music
fills our tiny room. Mrs. Kono has a small
record player. From this black, leather box,
with shining handles which we turn from time
to time, glorious music comes. In the hot,
burning oven, our Christmas chicken is cooking.
It sputters and makes funny noises. The lemon pies
father baked are already on the table. He has been
cooking all day. They look so nice,
my favorite pies. Only father can bake
such lovely, tasty pies. He must put magic
into them.

Father is an excellent cook. Before he became a gardener,
he worked as a chef in a big restaurant and in hotels.
And now, he still cooks on holidays or when we have
many guests. I love watching him cook. He never uses
a measuring cup, mostly his hands. He's always tasting,
making gurgling, funny noises in his throat
(for Japanese are allowed to make a lot of noise
when they eat; especially when they drink tea
or eat soup). Father closes his slanted eyes and
tastes it, then he gives me a tiny bit. He and mother
always treat me special, I guess because I'm
the youngest and not as strong as Yuki.

She doesn't mind; she knows I love her.
I watch my father cook and I listen.
The old song sounds full of joy....

Father ties a towel around his head. Mother hands
him a bowl. He raises his arm, dances around.
He is graceful as he waves his arm and bowl
in time with the music. We all laugh.
Mr. Kono joins him and sings. It is an old folk song.

Mother claps her hands in time with the rhythm.
She is looking at my slippers, the ones David
sent us for Christmas. She has a little smile.
I know her thoughts are with David;
this is the first Christmas he is not with us.
The music seems to grow louder. Little Kay-ko too
joins us. We all sing. Yuki, the Konos,
the whole room seems to fade. I see Japan.
The snow is gone. I see the happy rice planters
with their bright kimonos, their black hair tied
with printed towels, the gentle wind,
with lovely Mount Fuji, Fuji-san itself, in the distance.
The music, our voices, go beyond our house, out
into the snow, past the mountains and into space,
and this special day is made more magic,
and I know I shall remember it forever.

5

Our first spring
1943

March, April, how very quickly the winter months flew.
Spring is here. The harsh winter winds and snow slowly leave,
and the warm sun returns to the mountains and the hillsides.
There is a feeling of love in the air. I think this is my
favorite time of the year; aside, of course, from the summer
holidays. Father, Mr. Kono, everyone is clearing the surround-
ing land to start a vegetable garden. Neighbors help one another
to cut and uproot trees. The whole camp is so busy. Meanwhile,
I continue to go to school.

Kazuo, the boy who shares my desk at school,
is quiet. He is listening. We have a new teacher.
Miss Mizuno was transferred to teach another class.
Our class was too noisy and unmanageable, we were
told by our principal. So Miss Hamma stands before
us. She looks stern. The boys behave almost at once.
It was as if she carried an invisible stick.
I, too, become more interested in school.

Her voice reaches me:

"In Xanadu did Kubla Khan
A stately pleasure-dome decree;
Where Alph, the sacred river, ran
Through caverns measureless to man
Down to a sunless sea."

Coleridge's poem touches my imagination.
I look out the window. The sky is blue,
pale, yet so lovely. I can hear the birds too.
It is really spring. Our teacher's voice reaches me
again: "See if you can write poetry...write one with
six lines...every other word rhyming in the end."

Kazuo looks funny. He bends his dark head, looks
so serious. I write on a piece of paper, "Did you like
that poetry?" I pass the paper to him quietly. He
reads it and writes, "Yes," and returns it to me.
No one sees us. Miss Hamma is busy at her desk.
I look out the window again, the trees are
swaying gently.

Father's garden

Father has cleared most of the land around our house. We are
in the wilderness, so this is done with hard work. Every day
after work, he and Mr. Kono clear the trees and stumps.
Most of the Japanese people in Canada are farmers, or
gardeners like father. So they know exactly what
to plant and how. This morning, it seems that Yoko-san, our
neighbor across the street, is the only one who has not started
his garden. He is a big, burly man who lives with a woman and
her two young sons and a daughter, about my age. We all have
noticed the family keep to themselves. His back yard is
cleared for a garden but the front is left as it was. Is it because
he does not care to be seen? The boys are about Yuki's age or
older. We do not even know their names. They must be ill or
something, or they would not be allowed to stay with their
family but would have been taken away like David.

Father is planting seeds. The front of our house
is cleared; the dark, fluffy-looking soil is turned
and hoed. Father says after he plants the seeds here,
he will finish clearing the land in the back of the house
to plant corn and potatoes and lettuce.
It all sounds nice. Mother says, "This will help
us with the food. You know father makes
very little, only thirty-five cents an hour.

And that is because he's a foreman.
The others make twenty-five cents an hour,
hardly enough to pay for the expensive meat
and vegetables."

This Saturday everyone seems to be outside.
I can hear Mr. Kono singing to himself
as he plants the little seeds. His garden,
exactly the same size as ours, is on the
other side, so from the distance the two gardens
look quite nice, very neat. Later, father will plant
little fir trees on the end to separate our garden
from the dusty road. Mr. Kono will do the same
to make our homes look quite cozy.
I feel happy and I know mother is very pleased.

I squat and watch father. I do not speak
for I know he does not like to be disturbed
when he works. Mr. Kono's soft voice floats to us.
We listen. Father looks at me and winks.
I don't think Mr. Kono knows we are listening
to him sing. He is usually quiet and speaks very little.
He sounds so happy today.

"He has a good voice, Kono-san,
not like mine, flat." Father laughs softly.
He bends his lean, thin body and stamps
on the soil, covering the tiny, dark seeds well.
The upturned earth smells fresh. I take a deep breath.

"It smells nice," I exclaim. Father nods.
The sweat stands on his short-cropped black hair.
Some of it trickles down his dark, brown skin.
It is getting warm. The sun is smiling at us,
way in the sky. I know he is happy too.

Father stops, looks at the orange sun.
He turns, sees the old army veteran, Mr. Mori,
who had spit at him during the quarrel.
Now Mr. Mori waves his cane in greeting.
Father nods, smiles silently.
"Is he always so short-tempered as
that other night? " I ask. Father stares after him:
"He can't help it, I suppose. Doing this job,
watching over us like a spy for the R.C.M.P.
Of course, he and the others could have refused,
but some of them consider it an honor
to be working for the Government. It gives
them power. Of course, they like to pretend
they're representing us, that without them
we wouldn't be as well off. It makes them
feel better."

"When will the carrots grow? " I ask.
"Oh, in two, three weeks time. I hope it rains soon.
We need the water as well as the sun."
He mops his face. "How's school? Are you
learning anything? " "Fine," I reply.
"We have a new teacher, Miss Hamma.
Our class was so noisy, Miss Mizuno refused
to teach us any more." Father looks,
"I hope you are behaving! " His dark eyes
are serious. "You know, it's not easy
for those young girls to teach. They have had
no training, and I hear grade eight students
are almost impossible. If you don't like school,
at least learn to behave."

I look down, I feel bad. I talk quite a lot in school,
but most of the time, I just daydream out the
window. I hate mathematics, it bores me so much.
The only subjects I love are English and art,

but we have so little time to draw. I often
wonder why we can't do what we like. Kazuo
is good in math and he hates to draw.
I think this is so odd, not wanting to draw.
Yuki and I draw all the time.

"I'm bored at school," I tell father.
He looks, smiles, "I used to be like you, bored,
so I ran away from home, went to Manila
with my cousin. I was fifteen, he fourteen.
I think my mother had a fit. Then my cousin
caught malaria, almost died. We got so scared.
Our uncle sent us the money to return home.
We got real hell from my father; but a year
later, I ran off again, this time with mother's
blessing, to Canada. I never finished high school.
But this doesn't mean you're going to run off.
Times are different. You must finish school.
It's important for you; it's bad enough Yuki
can't finish high school."

"I won't run away." But I knew if I were
old enough, perhaps I would — just the way
father had. I touch the damp soil. The seeds are all
covered, waiting for the rain. I wish they would
hurry and grow. "Here comes Yuki." I look up.
Yes, there she is walking towards us with
little Kay-ko. Both are smiling. My sister
waves a letter. I stand up. "She has a letter, father."
I run towards them. Kay-ko shouts, "Big sister,
you have a letter with a picture of your brother."
"Really? " I ask, as I reach them. Yuki opens the letter.
I notice it is taped at one end, for the censors
always read our mail. "From David, Yuki? "
"Yes, take the photo, show dad and mom."

David smiles at us in the picture, he looks
so nice. Father looks, smiles, "He's grown,
seems older. Being alone does this.
Show mother." He wipes his brow again.
I can tell he is pleased. I run into the house.

Mother wipes her round glasses,
holds the picture. "Did this come with a letter? "
"Yes, Yuki has the letter. I think she's reading
it to dad...." She stares at the picture,
then quietly sits down, still holding it.
I feel she wants to be alone so I go outside again.
Kay-ko is sitting beside Yuki listening to her read,
"We are in a new camp. Schrieber,
Ontario is the nearest town. There are about
thirty boys, all about my age. Lots of
French Canadians where we are...."
We listen. Father looks worried. The letter ends.
Yuki gives it to me. I notice she has the
Vancouver *Province*, the newspaper.

"Tell mother about David. She's waiting."
Father says, "At least he is well.
This war....What does it say in the papers, Yuki? "
The daily paper from Vancouver is mailed to us.
It's two or three days old, but this is the only
way we know what is happening in the outside world....

After reading David's letter to mother, I return
outside. "I'm glad David had a chance to finish
high school." Father is speaking to Yuki.
Kay-ko is gone; she is watching *her* father
garden now. I sit on the steps beside Yuki
and listen. "You know, this war may last
for a long time. The Japanese are stubborn
and fierce fighters. They have that old samurai
tradition which the western people cannot understand."

Father speaks quietly; he looks at me. "Who knows
what will happen to all of us, as the war gets worse?
We are all scattered. They may even take us away again.
You must be prepared for the worst, Yuki.
You are old enough to understand. Shichan is
not too healthy. You must look after her,
and mother if...."

I look at Yuki. She nods, looks down at me.
I have never been very strong, have often
been in bed with severe colds and high temperatures.
Father used to tease me that I should carry a
hot water bottle and my bed with me.
If mother had not always watched over me
I know I would have perhaps died long ago.

Yuki looks concerned; "She hasn't caught
one of those bad colds for a while now."
"I think I'm getting stronger," I tell them.
Father looks, smiles. "Yes, I think you are.
We worried. I gave up hope sometimes,
but your mother was determined you would live.
You were born three months ahead of time.
We had no incubator. Mother placed you in a basket
all soft with cotton. You looked like a doll.
Then she put hotwater bottles around your little body."
"Did I cry? " I ask. "Yes, and you were always cold.
We put the basket near the window. I remember
the month of June that year was very warm.
The sun's rays helped you. But in the evening,
when the bottles cooled down, your tiny lips turned blue.
All night mother was up refilling the bottles with hot water."
"Really," I say, hoping to hear more. I look at Yuki.
She smiles, adds, "I remember one doctor came and fled."
"Why? " I ask. Father chuckles. "He took one look
at your tiny head and said, 'She won't last two days',

then left. He wouldn't even examine you."
Father lights a cigarette, inhales, continues. "Well, Shichan,
the two days have become many years, and you are
still with us." I look up at the sun. I feel close to him.

Yuki nudges me, adds. "You couldn't walk for a long time.
I used to carry you from place to place.
The bones in your hip didn't fit together right.

Then there was the operation in the hospital.
Does it still hurt? " I tell her no, only sometimes
when it's damp. Then I add, brightly,
"And I don't faint anymore, do I? "

"My God, you used to scare me," Yuki says
"You would be sitting in a chair, and all of a sudden
you would stop talking and would sort of disappear.
I mean you were there and yet you weren't.
Isn't that right, dad? " Father nods.
"Yes, we didn't know what to do. You would turn
chalk white, look as if you couldn't see us anymore
or hear us. It wasn't quite fainting, since your eyes
were open." Yuki asks, "Where did you go, Shichan? "
"I don't remember. I know I felt sad when I came back
and cried." "Yes, you would cry for hours. Poor mom.
She got so upset. She would call me, 'Hurry, Yuki,
get some ice cream and oranges. She loves them.
Maybe it will stop her from crying.'
So I'd run out to the corner store. What a child! "
"I remember that," I said, excited.
"Did I scare you? " "Yes, because after that
you would get one of those hair-raising fevers,
and you'd have to stay in bed for days."
Father nods. "You were some child. That's why
we spoiled you. Now, your legs are stronger.
I don't worry too much now. This dry air is good for you."

He smiles, "One thing about this camp,
we have wonderful air. It's a blessing
for the sick." Yuki says, "Yes, and don't worry.
I could work, and look after Shichan and mother."
She sighs and opens the paper. The headline reads:

"War with Japs...Heavy fighting continues...."

A terrible decision

I often wonder about this war. The Japanese are my father's
and mother's people. Strange to be fighting them. My father's
nephews are all in the army. We do not receive any letters from
our uncles and aunts in Japan and we do not know if they are
alive or not. Father does not speak of them much.

I ask father, "Why are we fighting? " "For land and
other things," father replies. "This is why we are here."
"But I'm not Japanese, like you. I was born here.
So were you." I look at Yuki. She says,
"That's nothing — a Jap is a Jap, whether you're born here
or not! " "Even if I change my name? "
"Yes, you look oriental, you're a threat." "A threat? Why? "
"God only knows! " Yuki replies. "It's mostly
racial prejudice, and jealousy. Remember we had
cleared the best land all along the Fraser Valley.
Good fisherman. This causes envy, so better to
kick us out. The damn war is just an excuse.
Dad knows. The West Coast people never liked
the orientals. 'Yellow Peril' is what they call us."

I look at father. "Yuki is speaking the truth," he says.
"This is why we had better return to Japan when we can."
Yuki looks surprised. "Return to Japan?
I don't want to go. What would I do there? "

In August is O-bon, the festival for the dead,
to wish joy for their souls and to remember them.

We wait for the train in small groups scattered
alongside the track. There is no platform.

I stare at the words "R.C.M.P. Office" all in red.
Their power seems to come through the very walls.

In the distance I see the Red Cross people with another
man. They stop to watch us with our buckets of water.

The bath-house is finally ready. We wash outside the tub,
rinse ourselves well before going into the hot water.

Japanese music is playing again to send us all home.
This evening, for a time, war and our problems are forgotten.

Someone is shouting,"Fire...fire...in road 'R'...hurry..."
The whole camp is out. Fear is in the night.

I go to the lake for the last time with mother to rinse our
clothes. She is singing, she looks so happy.

Father looks at us. "Would you rather stay in camps?
Be treated like dogs? You know you could never get
a decent job in Vancouver. Look at cousin Robert,
a university graduate, an honors student.
No one would hire him. So he's a gardener,
just like me. Is this what you want? To be always
a third-class citizen? I mind. I didn't come to this country
for this kind of treatment. Democracy! I'm a Canadian.

I have to pay all the taxes, but I have never been
allowed to vote. Even now, here, they took our land,
our houses, our children, everything.
We are their enemies. Don't you understand?
I have no desire to be part of this country.
There is no future for you here either. "

Yuki looks upset. "I know all that, but I still don't see
the point of going to Japan." Father looks annoyed.
"Japan is your parents' country.
All our relatives are there. There at least we will be free."
"Free? I wonder, what if they lose the war?
Anyway, I don't care if they do lose."
Yuki is angry now, "I refuse to go, that's all."
She stands up, walks into the house, slams the door.
Father wipes his hands on his pants. He, too, is angry now.
He stares at me, "One day, Shichan, you'll understand
all this. You must do as I say."

I feel strange. I don't want to leave here. I see
a small robin in the distance. He hops, skips gently,
puts his head close to the ground. He seems
to be listening. Then he picks into the soft ground,
and out he pulls a worm, then he flies quickly away.

Father is watching the bird too. He nods.
"Even that little robin is free. That is why

I want you to go to school. It's so important.
We couldn't fight the Government of Canada because
most of us have had little education. Do you understand? "
Father looks serious. I nod. Then, "Tell Yuki to come out.
She knows she mustn't slam the door in my face."
I hurry inside, Yuki goes out, for she knows
father could be very angry, and no one wants that.
I hear her crying outside, I feel so bad.
Mother looks out the window, but remains in the house.

She nods her head, continues to make the bread.
I watch her knead it with care. I love this bread.
She puts potatoes in.

Mother looks at me. "Is it about going to Japan? "
"Yes, Yuki doesn't want to go. Do you, mom? "
She sighs, dips her hands into flour.
"I have no one there... my sister and brother
are both in Canada. Life is hard there, in Japan.
I had a nice childhood, but we were not poor.
And for you to go to Japan, I wonder.
You are not as strong as Yuki. It would be
so difficult for you. You may not be able to walk
like other people, but you can learn to do other things.
Father doesn't realize that for you, for all you children
it's best to remain here. I don't listen to him when
he starts this. I know he's emotional and angry,
and I don't blame him, but.... Poor Yuki,
I pray something will happen to help us all."

The white, flour-covered dough is patted into shape.
She puts it by the window for the sun to leaven it,
covers it gently with a clean, white cloth,
looks out the window, "Yuki is running to Rose's.
No doubt, it is hard for her, her school unfinished,
living like this...."

That night, again, our house is quiet.
Father does not speak very much. Yuki hardly eats.
We all go to bed early. I do not even read
the new book I borrowed from my friend, Mary.
I stare into the dark night. "Yuki," I whisper,
"I'd go wherever you go." Yuki does not answer.
I do not know if she's asleep or just doesn't want
to talk. All is quiet.

Gifts from Japan!

Today all the Japanese in New Denver are to receive presents
from Japan. The Red Cross has organized it. We are all surprised.
I can't believe it, but Yuki says it's true. She says all the
Japanese in camps in Canada are getting some. I feel sad that we
are at war, and cannot write our thanks.

There has been a great shortage of our most prized food, soya
sauce and the special bean paste, *miso*. Mother uses this in her
cooking every day and lately we have run so short of it. Mrs.
Kono and mother have been diluting the soya sauce with brown
sugar. This makes the sauce taste smoky, but mother says,
"It's better than not having any at all." I know she is worried
what we will use, after we run out of it. She had remembered
to sneak several bottles in her baggage along with the paste
which we use for soup, the main staple of many Japanese
families.

Now today, this wondrous news. The people in Japan, hearing
how we have been treated by the Canadian Government,
and that we are living in camps in the woods,
send us barrels of soya sauce and *miso* paste.
Can you imagine! I am so happy over this;
now, Mrs. Kono and mother don't have to worry.

But grownups are funny. Instead of being pleased,
they have a big argument. Some of the elderly
and a few of the younger ones shout that we shouldn't
accept this food. "Food from the enemy! "
Others say, "We are treated as traitors and enemies
of Canada, so we should take it with thanks."
Finally, the food is accepted and distributed carefully
to each family. Father says with a bitter smile,
"The Canadian Government treats us like dogs,
but the country we left to come here still cares about us."

Miso paste, all dark orangy, and smelly, arrives for
mother and Mrs. Kono. So do several bottles of
soya sauce. We look at it with great happiness.
The dark liquid looks so lovely in the bottle.
Mother and Mrs. Kono keep on saying, "A blessing
from Heaven." I see Mrs. Kono carefully place a small
bit of *miso* paste in a tiny dish and a few drops of
soya sauce in a round Japanese sake cup and place them
on her Buddhist altar. She always does this before dinner,
offers part of the food to Lord Buddha as a gesture
of thanks. I think it is very nice to have a little
altar like that and pray to one's God.

6

Early summer 1943
Water at last!

June arrives, and with it, water! At last, water is piped into the
main streets of the whole camp. It is hard to believe. All spring
I watched the men lay the long, shining pipes, then put in little
taps, one for each eight or nine houses. We still have to go outside to draw water but now we do not have to walk so far. Our
tap is quite close to our house. It will be especially good for the
old people. They found it so hard to fetch water. Often, the
younger boys brought it for them. Father is pleased. He fought
so hard for this.

I look at the pipe with the small, shining tap.
It appears from the ground like a metal snake.
I wonder if it will really work. Slowly, I turn it.
A pause, then the clear water gushes out.
It crashes down into the narrow wood sink
placed flush to the ground. I shout, "It works!" The water
keeps pouring out. Mrs. Kono is standing
with her two buckets. "My," she exclaims, "it's like
a dream. One forgets so quickly that we had water
in our homes at one time. Isn't this wonderful,
Shichan?" We smile at each other with pure happiness.
I touch it with my hands, let it flow through my fingers.

Little Kay-ko comes running at the sound of the water.
She shrieks with glee, we all laugh.
Mrs. Kono fills her buckets. The clear, clear water
dances in the round metal buckets.
Mrs. Kono says softly, "We must thank Kuan-non San.
God is merciful, after all. We are grateful."

Our neighbor from across the street comes
swinging her buckets. Mrs. Nishimura has lost all
her teeth, but she always smiles. I wonder why

she doesn't wear her false teeth. Today she
opens her mouth in a wide, wide grin.
Kay-ko stares, laughs. It does look funny.
A big, dark hole. "We must all thank the men. "
She lisps, "If they didn't appeal to the Red Cross,
goodness knows we mightn't have even a roof
over our heads. Shichan, a miracle for your young
heart. We must thank Lord Buddha." Mrs. Kono
is all smiles. "We must always fight for our rights
as women, too." I hear all the taps
pouring the water out. It sounds lovely.

Mother comes with her pot of rice.
"My," she beams, then bends and washes the rice.
Swish, swish, her right hand swirls the wet
rice. It makes a funny, familiar sound.
"We must never again take our water for granted."

Mother looks serious and sighs, straightens herself.
"I heard Mrs. Takeda say they are going to build
a bath-house closeby now that we have water.
Did you hear? " Mrs. Nishimura asks mother. She grins.
"Yes, my husband was talking about it last week.
Then we won't have to walk so far to bathe. A blessing! "
All nod, and agree, "A blessing indeed." Mrs. Nishimura
cackles, "Ahee, it was hard for me to walk so far in the
snow. My husband thought I had lost my mind,
but I can't sleep unless I have my hot bath! "
I stare into her face. Her dark eyes squeeze
together, and she laughs. We all start laughing again.
Mrs. Nishimura swings her buckets, half full.
She spills most of the water as she crosses the street.
"Ahee, it's a good thing the water is close...
and we don't have to pay for it." With this,
she vanishes into her tiny house.

Yoko-san, his daily morning prayer

One early, early morning, soon after the water is piped in the
front street, I awake. I hear strange sounds. I lie very still,
listening. The sound is coming from the outside. Splash...splash...
sound of water... then a Buddhist prayer. I turn to see if Yuki is
still asleep. She is.

I rise quietly and jump down from my bed.
Mother is up; the big, shining kettle is singing.
Mother wonders why I'm up so early.
"Your father and Kono-san have just left for the mountains
to cut logs. Can't you sleep, Shichan?"
"That funny noise woke me," I reply, as I go
to the front window. I peek out the window.
Outside, I see the strangest sight.
It's Yoko-san, our neighbor from across the street.
He is sitting cross-legged right inside the narrow
wood sink, without any clothes except a small cloth
in the middle. He has a small bucket and is splashing
water over his head. Yoko-san's eyes are closed tightly.
His thick lips move without stopping. He's praying...
then...splash, splash. The cold water pours over him.
His thick, heavy body is shiny and wet.
I stare, fascinated. I remain still.

Mrs. Kono comes to the window. She sees Yoko-san
and becomes very annoyed. She says,
"Takashima-san, Yoko-san is a nuisance.
He does this almost every morning
and for fifteen minutes. I need water
but I daren't go out. It's indecent. The barbarian!
My husband and I are Buddhist but we don't believe in
displaying our religion, and in such a manner!
It's a disgrace. Ah, I can't stand to look.
How can that woman live with him?

We should report him to the Police."
Mother joins us at the window, she nods her head,
"A strange man. He usually does this earlier,
before the men leave for work. He must have slept in.
Better not to stare at him."

I ask mother, as I move away still staring,
"Mom, why does he pour water over his head? "
Mother smiles, "I suppose it's like baptism.
Water is a purifier. I agree with Kono-san,
it's wrong to do this in public. It is vulgar. "
As I move away from the window, I see the praying man
stand up, pick up his bucket and the towel he uses
to rub himself, step out of the tiny sink, walk quietly
across the street. The morning sun is just appearing
from the eastern hills. His thick, wet body looks unreal.
He silently disappears into his half-hidden house.
As soon as he is gone, women come rushing out
with their buckets, including Mrs. Kono.
I guess they were waiting for him to finish his prayers.
I sit at the table and close my eyes. I try to shut the man
from my head. I do not care to think of him anymore....

Later in the day, I bump into the young girl
who lives in the house with him. I stare at her.
I wonder what she thinks of Yoko-san
splashing water and praying. I feel funny,
but I do not run away. I think her name is
Yuri-ko. She smiles shyly, whispers "Hello."
I smile back, "Hi, Yuri-ko." But her eyes
are not really smiling, and before I can say anything else
she walks quickly past me. I stare after her.
The little pig-tails on each side of her dark head
bob up and down. She looks so lonely.
She does not even go to school anymore.
She is only about two years older than I am.

She has never played with us. I see, though, she has a very
gentle face, and behind her round steel-rimmed glasses
her eyes look so sad. I remember now, we never see
her or her family at any of the public gatherings.
I feel bad as I walk away from her.
And I am glad father doesn't rush out and splash
water, for he's still a Buddhist even if mother is not.
I am glad, too, mother lets me play with other children.
I'd cry every night if I couldn't go to school
and be with my friends, even if I complain sometimes....

June: our garden grows

Yuki tends the garden often. It is easier now, since we have
water so closeby. The bath-house is ready too, and as the sun
becomes warmer, the vegetables need more water.

I see Yuki watering our garden. She is pouring
water over the young corn at the back of the house.
I join her. School is just finished for the day.
I watch for a while, then I pick up the small tin
with little holes in the bottom, dip it into the bucket
and hold it over the lettuce. I am not watching
carefully so I spill some of the water in the wrong place.
Yuki sees this, "Good God, can't you be more careful?
You're wasting most of the water." I stare at her.
She looks annoyed. I screw up my face.
I drop the tin, walk away, angry and hurt.
Yuki says, "Little brat, it's your garden, too."
I go to the front of the house and sit on the steps.

Kay-ko comes and sits with me. I ignore her
for awhile, then she nudges me and smiles.
I soon forget my anger, and return her smile.

She looks so pretty in her little red dress with lace.
Mother sees us, "Can't you help your sister water
the garden? Surely, this isn't too much?"
I look at her; her face shows concern.
"You must learn to help her. You are not a baby."

I slowly rise. Kay-ko says, "I'll help you."
"All right, mother." I walk to the back once more,
with Kay-ko. Yuki is still watering the corn.
She ignores me. I pick up the tin again.
I hold it close to the lettuce. This time I do it
more carefully. The leaves of a lettuce gently
curl as the water falls on its face.

Summer 1943
Swimming

Because we started school so late, we had to go until
the third week in July. Finally, at last, school is finished, and I
now go swimming almost every day. Such fun!

The lake is still and calm. On the other side the tall,
rugged mountains, snow capped, are reflected
on the glasslike water. I feel the small, gray gravel
under my bare feet. I curl my feet into it.
It feels rough but nice. Kay-ko holds my hand.
She looks at the water, dips her tiny, round toes,
squeaks. Yuki and I laugh. She *is* funny.

"It's cold," she whispers. I whisper back, "Is it?
Maybe we should warm it." Kay-ko chuckles.
My friend Mary joins us. She is tall for her age.
She puts down her belongings, stands away from the
water. Mary grins, "You go in first, I'm slow."

Yuki jumps in. We all scream as she splashes us.
"Don't be a big baby. Come on. You won't die."
I release Kay-ko's hand and wade in.
The cold water is strange. I feel nice and cool.
I look down. I stare. "My legs look broken, funny. "
Yuki laughs. "The sun's rays do this."
With a jerk she pulls my legs. I go under,
roll in the water, sputter, come up again. I can't see.
The water is up my nose. Everybody laughs.
I start to laugh.

I am not afraid of the water....We had lived by the sea in
Vancouver. I had gone swimming every day there too, and I
loved to play in the sand, especially when the tide was out. My
friends and I used to hunt tiny, baby crabs. We'd turn the wet
stones over; the crabs used to rush out from their hiding place,
their legs moving quickly and their claws and eyes waving in
the air. We just did this for fun. I never killed them. Father
went crab hunting in Vancouver. He put them in a big pot. I
watched him boil them. Some were still alive. They tried to
crawl away. I felt so bad, I ran out of the house, didn't come
home for supper. Mother said I was too sensitive. Later, she
made me an omelet.

I return to Kay-ko and take her hand.
She flips on her stomach, and paddles with her feet.
She's all wet now. Mary joins us. We all splash and scream.
I see the round, round sun high above.
The sky is clear, blue. I hear laughter of other children
not far from us. I look at the sun, wondering how
long it has been there. I turn on my back,
shout to the sun, "Hello, sun! "
We all shout, "Hello, sun! " It seems to grow larger
as I stare at it, and the blue sky seems to grow
a blue, blue, and I seem to fly up and touch the sun
and the lovely sky....

Day of the festival

My people, the Japanese, are very creative people. Many are
carpenters, gardeners, landscape-gardeners like my father, and
amateur dancers and actors, so we have many concerts and
plays, and many festival celebrations. The one held in August
is called "O-bon" — a festival for the dead, to wish joy for their
souls and to remember them....

On the day of festival O-bon I go to the square
with Mary, my friend. Colored lanterns are strung
around the enclosed square. Already people are
gathered in a circle. There is a magic feeling
of excitement in the air. The gay-colored dancers
with ribbons in their hair gather at the far end.
Their different patterned kimonos look lovely in the dusk.
"There's Rose," I whisper to Mary.
"She is your sister's friend? "
"Yes, she studied dancing in Japan and teaches
the young girls. She is very good. Watch her."

More people gather. There is a wood platform
built at the center of the square with colored lanterns
and paper flowers all around it. The microphone
is placed in the front. Music starts.
It is a familiar O-bon song. The dancers
are lined in a row. The smallest children
are at the front, the very smallest is not much older
than Kay-ko. She looks like a doll. Their teacher begins
to move her arms and legs. All follow her.
They look so lovely. Then a woman steps
to the microphone. She begins to sing.

Great shouts of joy ring out from the old people's lips.
They love these songs so much. We all clap our hands.
The singer's lusty, throaty voice fills the air.

The dancers are near us now, they all dance in
equal rhythm, forming a circle. Around they dance.
They look like birds, so lovely. The sleeves of
their kimonos bellow out. I see Rose and smile at her.
Her arms form the shape of the universe and her hands,
the sun. All the dancers do likewise. All sing the song.
Some clap their hands. We imitate the movements
of the dancers' arms. I feel the departed spirits
must be watching us. The happy sun is slowly sinking.
The mountains turn bright purple; they seem on fire.
The half-hidden orange fire lingers,
sorry to leave this lovely dance.
Then far on the other side of this splendid sky
I see the pale, pale moon watching, silvery and ghostly.

A man is singing now, a harvest song.
The dancers look different now in the dusky light.
They seem to be floating. I walk away.
Mary follows. We go to the lake.
In the early moonlight the water looks so different.
We do not speak. The lake is still, mirrorlike.
We sit. The music reaches us, touches the moon.

The bath-house

The bath-house is finally ready. It is not too far from our house.
It is made of wood, of course, and built the same way as the old
Japanese baths, the women's section on one side, the men's on
the other. Only a thin wall separates the two sections. It is a
community bath. We all wash outside the tub, rinse ourselves
well before going into the hot water....

The steam rises slowly from the big, rectangular tub.
The hot, hot air fills the misty room.

The woman next to me sighs. It's Mrs. Nishimura,
our neighbor. The water touches her shoulders.
She moves her arms and sighs. Her eyes are closed;
her lips move. She rubs her face with her cloth,
sighs again. I see her flat, empty breasts.
They float in the water as two squashed balloons.
They look funny. Yuki nudges me, whispers,
"Stop staring." I grin at her, I stifle a laugh.
"Mom's aren't like that," I tell Yuki, "How come? "
She shrugs her shoulders, looks away. I still stare.
The old woman snaps open her black eyes, looks at me.
She has heard and she chuckles. "One day, child,
yours will be like this, after you have had many,
many children. Ah, you young ones. So innocent! "
Her empty mouth opens, her eyes twinkle.

I look down at my child-body; it seems so
different from hers. I look around.
I see other old women, with sunken jaws
and flat, empty breasts. They all splash about,
the young and the old, washing each other's backs.
The children make lots of noise, their firm,
little bodies shining with water.
I see at the other end of the large room,
gossiping women sitting, talking, talking.

Yuki, I know, dislikes them for doing this.
So does mother, for she seldom gossips
and says nasty things about people. We usually go early
in the afternoon before the gossip-crazy women arrive,
but today even though it is quite early,
a few are already sitting on their usual benches,
half nude or nude, just watching, eyes moving,
tongues moving. Yuki says, "Don't look at them.
They are evil. To sit like that and just speak terrible
things about their neighbors. And just think,

60

they waste so much time. " I turn away.
I sink myself way deep into the hot water.
It gradually relaxes me and my body begins
to tingle all over. It *is* nice.

Summer night

Our toilets are outside, so during the night I often find myself
standing under the great, vast sky.

I stand still. I look up, the stars are close.
In this late summer night, the crickets are singing.
They fill the warm, scented air with their songs.
The bullfrogs join in. I see fireflies dart here
and there, their tiny lights like magic.
I stare up into the sky. It's deep, dark blue.
I see a handsome knight in search of a lovely
princess with long gold hair; she is lost somewhere
in this vast sky, and only one star knows where
the evil magician and his helpers have hidden her.

I hear someone. I turn, gasp. It's mother. I stare at her.
Mother laughs quietly, "Are you imagining things
again? You shouldn't stand outside like this.
It's very late. I was wondering where you had gone? "
She comes closer, stares into the night sky too.

We both listen to the night music of the insects
and the frogs. Far away wild coyotes are howling.
The whole camp is asleep. Mother speaks,
"David is sleeping, too." "I dreamt about him," I tell her.
"Last night. We were in Vancouver again. He was
gathering wood for us. It all seemed so real, mother."
She takes my hand. In the dark I can tell

she is pleased. "We will hear from him soon.
He has not written for a while." We slowly walk
into the house and close the door,
shutting the lovely night from us.

7

Fall 1943
High school for Yuki

In the fall, Yuki is able to continue her high school. She enters
grade twelve. She is quite happy. The Catholic Sisters of Notre
Dame des Anges, with Father Clement as supervisor, started
this high school for the older students. The classes are held in
the nuns' former home near the village of New Denver. Yuki
shows it to me. It is a large wooden house, painted and neat, with
tiny verandas at the front. It looks very cozy.

"How is school, Yuki? " I ask.
She has all her large text books on the table.
She looks up. The late afternoon light is on her face.
Everything looks orangy and nice. "Oh, fine."
"The Sisters, they speak English well? " "Of course,
silly: Did you think they spoke Japanese? "
"I saw three Sisters in the drugs the other day.
Mary and I noticed they spoke only French."
Yuki laughs, looks at me: "They are all bilingual.
They speak both French and English."
"Is that what 'bilingual' means? "
"Yes, you speak two languages, Japanese and English.
So you're bilingual too." I smile.

I look at all her books. She's studying Shakespeare.
"Do you like school? "
Yuli smiles. "It's great to be with girls my own age."
"Are there any boys? "
"Yes, but all younger than Rose and me.
They're all in grade nine, two in ten."
"There's only twenty students? "
"Yes, and they all study like mad. They're so
happy that school has started again. So am I.
We have central heating and electricity,
and long desks with benches. Four students sit

at each desk. It's quite nice and comfortable."
"Ah! Ours is so cold, and we get those stupid
correspondence courses. We have to answer
hundreds of questions. It doesn't make sense.
I don't understand any of them. I wish
I were older, then I could go to high school."

But then I remember something. "Do you pray often
with the nuns, Yuki? " Surprised, she asks, "Pray?
Why do you ask that? " "Well, people are saying
you will become a Catholic one day.
You have to pray with them and everything. "
Yuki is quiet. She looks angry. "On the first day,
Sister St. Rita, our principal, spoke to us:
'We will respect the religion of each of you
and we ask you to respect ours.' She told us
they didn't begin the school to spread
their religion, that help was needed
because of the war. 'We do say the Lord's Prayer
every morning before class,' she said.
'I do not ask you to repeat the prayer after me,
but I'd like you all to please stand while I say it.'
That's all she said, and we do this every morning.
It's not asking too much, is it? "
I think about it. I feel better. "No," I answer.

Father enters the house. "Well, another fall.
It's getting cold. Did you pick the corn, Yuki? "
He rubs his hands. "Yes, it's near the sink.
Peel it, Shichan. Do I have to tell you each time? "
Yuki scolds me, so I start to peel the fresh corn.

They are all green and sweet smelling in a big bucket.
I take the long gold silklike husk
and pull it. It comes off, and inside is the little
yellow pearllike corn. All in neat little rows.

I look at them. I line the cobs neatly on the
wooden sink. In the pale, late autumn light
they do look lovely. Yuki comes and puts them
in a big pot. Soon they'll be eaten and I'll forget
all about them. And it took so long for them to grow.
Yuki watered them so often. Father says:
"I guess that's the last of it." Yuki begins to cook.
"Are we ever going to have electricity? " she asks.
Father says, angry, "We're working on it now.
Mr. Sumi and I saw the Commissioner today.
You know Sumi-san speaks perfect English;
he went to university in Toronto.
I told the Commissioner my daughter's eyes
are ruined. You know what he answered?
'I can't help that. This is wartime! '
Sumi-san told him then, 'We pay rent for the houses,
but we've no electricity, not enough heating,
and no water in them. None of us ever hurt Canada.
I'm a naturalized citizen, so are many of us.
You even charge us taxes. It's wrong to treat us
like enemies. It's unjust. We're only asking
for our rights.' You know what Mr. Baldwin answered?
He said: 'You are in camps. Therefore you are all
considered enemies. You have no rights.' "
Father clenches his fist. "I was so mad I would have
hit him, if it wasn't for Sumi-san. He nudged me quickly.
He knows me so well. He knows how mad I can get."

"Maybe if one of us went blind," I say hopefully,
"they'd put the electricity in." Yuki makes a face.
"And what good would that do? Really, you say the
dumbest things! " Father ignores us, continues,
"We wrote another letter to the Red Cross.
Calling us 'enemies of Canada' for no reason
but to justify taking our property, houses,
belongings, our children and our *dignity*.

Do you blame the older people for wanting
to return to Japan? " Yuki is silent.
She hangs on tight to her silence.
Then, "Where's mother? " she asks me.
"Gone to the bath-house," I reply.
Father rubs his dark hair: "I think I'll go too,
to hear the latest news. I'll be home for supper."
He goes out with his towel. Yuki is silent again.
She quietly cuts the beans into nice small pieces,
then the carrots, the meat. She is a good cook,
and does it quickly. She is always efficient
and knows how to do things. The sun is going down.
"Yuki, look, the sky, isn't it lovely! "
Yuki looks up. "Yes, we may not have luxury,
but we sure have nature. " And the last rays
of the dark gold-red sun begin to fade.

A sad parting

The United Church of Canada has begun a high school, too.
Yuki says it is not as nice as the Catholic one. The Anglican
Missionaries want Yuki to change schools and go to it. They
come to visit mother, but mother says if Yuki likes the Catholic
school better and is happy there, no need to change. School has
started for me too. Grade Seven. I find it dull as usual. To make
matters worse, I don't like the girl who shares the desk with me.
She isn't too smart and talks a lot, mostly about herself, and
asks silly questions.

I am sitting at the back of the class.
Kazuo is way at the front. I miss him.
I miss my window too. Lily talks all the time.
We have Miss Mizuno again. No one wants our class.
We don't mind. I like Miss Mizuno.

Lily leans over and starts to whisper again.
I draw away, but her face follows mine. She says
"I heard Kazuo's leaving for Japan with his family."
I stare at her, I wonder if she's lying. I feel funny.
"When? " I ask. "I don't know." "Didn't he tell you? "
"No." Slyly, "Too bad." Her dark eyes stare into mine.
I look down into my books, I can't seem to focus.
Why is Kazuo leaving? Will we have to leave, too?
I long to run out of the room....

At noon, on the way home, I stop Kazuo and
ask him if he is really leaving for Japan....
He looks at me, then away. He gives his funny smile,
shy-like, "Yes, in February or in early spring, a
boat is coming to Vancouver. So my mother said."
"But why? You're a Canadian. Can't you stay? "
"I can, but I have no one aside from my family.
I'm only twelve. My father wants to return
so he asked the Government. My older brother is
a soldier with the Japanese Army in Burma.
Grandmother is getting old. She has a farm and no one to help.
Dad thinks it's better. We will be able to work,
and we will be free. I don't want to go, but I
don't know what to do. I can't run away, can I?
We're in camps...." He turns and walks quickly away.
"I'm sorry. I'll miss you," I say, but I don't think he heard.
I hurry home. I feel very sad. Nothing makes sense
in this life. I know I may never see him again.
Japan is so far away.

Late fall

The New Denver area was especially chosen by the Provincial
Government because of its high altitude and dry air. Here, the
Japanese people built the T.B. sanatorium to take care of their

own sick, as the Government had planned. It is completed within a year of our moving to the camp. It is built near the lake, and one side of the hospital overlooks the lake and the mountains. It is a lovely, small hospital, for many of our people. The hospital is staffed by our own doctors and nurses. During the day, I see patients resting in the quiet garden which surrounds the other side of the hospital. I do not ever enter the hospital even on a visit, for we know no one there, but I hear that several of our friends' relatives are patients.

Father goes with some men to gather ferns, herbs and mushrooms. They take a boat, cross the lake, climb the mountains. Father is very good at this, for he is nimble and has keen eyes. I do not like the mushrooms even though they are considered great delicacies.

Mother looks. "You are a strange child.
You don't like mushrooms, crabs, any fish except salmon.
How do you expect to grow? Mushrooms are good for you. "
I wrinkle my nose. The house stinks of mushrooms.
Mother and father are preserving them for the winter.
"For heavens sake, can't you even try a piece? "
Father is annoyed. I lean over the big, blue pot.
It is bubbling over. "I don't like the smell. It makes
me sick." Yuki stares at me. "You're a spoilt brat.
That's all! " I feel bad, but really, it does make me ill.
I make a face and run towards the door.
"What are we going to do with that child?
No wonder she's always ill. She never eats anything,
except eggs." I hear father speaking as I go out. I turn.
The house seems to dance with the smell of mushrooms.

Homebrew

Father, like other Japanese people, loves to drink. We cannot
buy any liquor in our camps. The Government thought drinking
could cause riots. But this does not stop father and his friends.
They begin to make their own brew, sometimes with rice, other
times with fruits. Father now has a big barrel full of oranges,
raisins, mixed with brown sugar. It is considered a "heavenly
drink" by father, but "poison" by mother who does not drink at
all. Nor does she even like the smell....

Father takes the long, big wooden spoon
which he has made, opens the barrel lid and mixes
the fermenting fruits. A strong sweet-sour smell
comes out of the barrel. It makes us sick. I stare into
the barrel. It is all bubbling and seems to be alive.
"It's getting mellow, it will be ready soon,"
father beams. Mother sighs and nods,
but does not say anything. She has learned not to....

Tonight father's friends come to taste the wine.
All smack their lips; father does not think it is
quite ready. Mr. Shimizu says he likes it like this,
a bit raw. In the end they drink quite a lot of it.
Mother laughs, says, "This is one thing they can't
wait until it's ready. What a habit to get into."
She does not taste it, but serves food for the men.
Slowly, we notice they are getting quite tottery.
As always when this happens they stop talking
and start to sing. They forget about their problems.
Father gets up and dances. Mr. Shimizu sings,
beats his chopsticks on the plate, his eyes closed.
The Japanese songs start pouring out of his lips.
I watch, mother claps her hands.
Before one knows what is happening, we all
join them. This is lots of fun.

And as the evening progresses, they say
the not-so-ready brew tastes better and better.
It is early morning before the guests stagger out
of our little house, all shouting and laughing.
I am in bed by then, and listen to the noise
as the happy men totter home to their families....

8

Christmas 1943

It is now over a year since we were moved from Vancouver.
Sometimes, I do wonder if ever we will see a big city again. I
still miss the busy streets, the movie theaters. We see films in an
old hall in the village, but it is not the same; the film stops every
half hour, and breaks down. But Yuki says it's better than
nothing. The people in New Denver still do not speak to us. We
just stare at each other. Funny, though, they let us go to their
church, even bake cakes for their bazaars, but they do not ever
visit our camps or our houses....

It is Christmas time again!
Yuki tells me about the Christmas party she attended.
"...We all sat at a long table. The long candles
were lit and in front of each place was a
gold shoe, with the student's name on it. See, this
is the gold shoe." I stare. It is in the shape of a
Dutch shoe and it is covered with gold rice.
It really, really, sparkles.

"Did all the students get one? "
"Yes, and look, Shichan, there's candies and nuts inside.
See? And here is the little tie to lace the shoe.
The Sisters made them. Can you imagine? "
I peer inside. The little chocolate candies
and brown nuts are there, like a treasure chest.
"Then what happened? " I ask, for I want to know
every detail. Yuki smiles. "Oh, Father Clement
was there at the head of the table. He said a short
prayer, then we began to have our dinner. It was
so lovely, the table. In the center was a huge
log-tree cake, a cake shaped like a log, complete
with an axe made of icing right in the middle.
Sister Gemma made it. All of the Sisters and
Father looked so happy, and we could feel this

happiness. They really try to make us feel
warm, you know."

"Was the cake good? " "Yes, Sister Gemma is a
professional cook. We had cold roast turkey, cold
meats and salads, vegetables. Then we sang songs."
I close my eyes for a moment. I can see it all.
"See, Shichan, open your eyes." I do. I see paper
cut like a Christmas tree, several pages, and typed
inside are Christmas carols. Some of the pages
are of different colored paper. Yuki places it
on the table to show me: the tree stands on its trunk.
"They are really kind," Yuki says, "all the Sisters
and Father Clement. And not one word of Jesus
was mentioned at dinner, and it's *Christ*mas! "
I close my eyes again. I see Sister Raphael clearly,
just like that Saturday afternoon a week ago,
her big, warm, twinkling eyes when she smiles —
I notice that these Sisters do not shave their heads.
Their hair shows a bit from their starched
caplike coverings, and their black beads from their
wrists rattle in the wind. Their black stockings
and shoes are visible under their black heavy capes.
I hear Sister Raphael's voice, "And what grade are you in? "
I wish I were in grade eight, then I could go
to their school. I want to say this, but I remain quiet.
I look down and say "Grade seven." I somehow say it
too loud and it sounds as if I am angry.
I turn red, feel awful; I look up.
The Sisters are grinning. They don't seem to mind.
Yuki pokes me; she says hurriedly,
"Well, good-bye, Sisters. It was nice to see you.
We must be going." "Good-bye, Yuki, see you
Monday, and your sister...bye...
perhaps you would like to come to see
the school one day? " I stare. "Oh,yes! May I?

Our school is terrible! " They laugh, and Yuki
drags me away before I can say anything else.

"Shichan," Yuki's voice comes softly. "Shichan."
My mind has wandered. "Yes," I reply.
"Would you like to have the gold shoe? "
I stare at her. I touch the gold candy-filled shoe
gently. I beam. "Oh, yes."

"Well, you may, and the little paper tree.
I am sorry you could not be at the party too."
I look at her. I feel so happy.

9

Spring 1944

The war with Japan is getting very bad. I can feel my parents
growing anxious. There is a lot of tension in the camp; rumors
of being moved again, of everyone having to return to Japan.
Kazuo and his family leave for Japan. Many are angry they have
left us. Some call them cowards, others call them brave! I only
feel sad, for I liked Kazuo so much, so very much.

Father shouts at mother, "We return to Japan! "
"But what are we going to do? You have your brothers
and sisters there. I have no one. Besides, the children...."
"Never mind the children," father answers.
"They'll adjust. I'm tired of being treated as a spy,
a prisoner. Do what you like; I'm returning! "

I can see Mrs. Kono looks confused.
"My husband is talking of returning to Japan, too.
I think it's the best thing. All our relatives
are still there. We have nothing here."
Yuki stares at her. "It's all right for you, Mrs. Kono,
you were born there, but we weren't.
I'm not going. That's all! "
And she walks out of the house.

Mother gets very upset. I know she wants to cry.
"I don't want to go to Japan, either," I say.
"They're short of food and clothing there.
They haven't enough for their own people.
They won't want us back."

All of a sudden I hate that country for having started
the war. I say aloud, "Damn Japs! Why don't they
stop fighting? " Father glares. "What do you mean 'Japs'?
You think you're not a Jap? If I hear you say that again
I'll throttle you. " I see anger and hatred in his eyes.

I leave the room, go out of the house. I hear him
say loudly to mother, "It's all your fault. You poison
our children's minds by saying we're better off here."

And another argument starts. I am getting tired
of it, and confused. I feel so helpless, and wish
again I were older, then maybe I could go somewhere....
But I do not hate the people in Japan. I know
Yuki doesn't hate them either, really.
It's all so senseless. Really, maybe children should
rule the world! Yuki tells me it is wrong for father,
because of his anger at the wrong done towards him
and us, to expect us to return to his country:
"Sure, we're Japanese. But we think like Canadians.
We won't be accepted in Japan if we go there."

A gift from David

David and many of the young men in camps in Ontario and
other parts of eastern Canada are allowed to move out of the
camps, but not, of course, back to the West Coast. So
David moves to Toronto. We are all very happy for him,
especially mother and Yuki. He writes to us. He is able to
find a job in a machine shop. Some parts of the letter are
funny....

"...people in Toronto ask me where I learned to speak
English so well. I tell them I went to school in Vancouver,
that many of us have. They stare and say, 'But what about
all those stories about your people being ignorant, not
speaking the language and not living like Canadians?'
Well, they look at me and are amazed that I don't wear samurai
clothes. Can you believe it? This is what propaganda does! ..."

I am almost thirteen now and I read and write English.
Yuki and I laugh. Really, *they* are ignorant.

David sends us many nice presents from Toronto. Now that he
is working, he writes, he would like to share his good fortune
with us. Mother is pleased and so is father. He even manages to
send us boxes of chocolates, and they are so scarce here.

David sends Yuki and me a wallet each.
Mine is made of black leather with a shining zipper
which closes all around the wallet. I am so happy,
the day I receive it, I put it by my pillow
before going to sleep. Father sees me and says,
"You're an old woman, taking your gold to bed!
Look, mother, that child is taking her gold to bed! "
He laughs. I pretend not to hear and put the black
treasure under my pillow. Yuki laughs too,
"You're so funny. Honestly, my God," she sighs.

Early in the morning while everyone is asleep,
I take out my wallet, slowly open it. The small
picture of my brother is still there; he had put
it in before sending it to us. I open the change section.
I have forty cents, money mother has given me
for helping with the chores. Everything is in place.
I zip the zipper back in its place, smell the leather.
It smells fresh and nice. I whisper, "Thank you, David,"
and slowly, I feel myself drifting off to another world.
My arms and legs seem to grow large, large.
They go beyond the room, through the walls,
across the road, through the trees beyond the lake
and even touch the mountains. I feel as if I am a giant.
Then I go very quickly into space
and see different colored spots of light.
They are very beautiful. And now my body is gone.

76

I leave it behind, and I go faster and faster
at a great speed. The colored spots of light are gone,
and I am in a pale blue, lovely space, very airy
and magiclike! This happens so often,
I am used to it now. But when I was younger,
I used to get scared and force myself to wake up.
Now I love the feeling of flying!
And I love the color dreams, where I see all
my old friends, and David. Even my dead grandma
comes to see me, or I go to see her.
We have tea together. It is fun. She still wears
long, black shoes with laces past her ankles, just the
way she always did, and narrow, dark dresses.

I tell mother the next day. She had told us
that bad dreams should be told to someone immediately
and treasured dreams kept, like found money,
to oneself. But this one we all feel happy about,
to know grandma is well and is looked after.

Mother always dreams in color, too. She told us
that the night before a telegram which she was
expecting for so long arrived from Canada
(this was when she was still in Japan), she dreamt
of Fuji-san. Mount Fuji is a holy mountain in Japan,
and to see it in one's dreams brings good luck.
And true enough, the telegram read that her papers
were all in order, so she could sail for Vancouver.
She said this was one of her most joyous days.
Isn't it lovely? Father says we are a bit crazy,
always dreaming and talking about our dreams,
but mother and I don't pay any attention,
for the dreams keep appearing, and we believe in them.

Kabuki plays

The Japanese people are indeed very creative. A group from another camp at Sandon, about ten miles from ours, comes to perform Kabuki plays for us. They tour the other camps, all within thirty miles distance. This is done every eight or ten months. My, but mother and father and all the old people love it. Father says in his province of Fukuoka, the people were great theater lovers. When he was a child, the whole family would arise early in the morning and walk for miles to see a Kabuki. It would last all day, and everyone came home late.

"Kabuki
March 18 to March 21
Performance, 8 o'clock sharp"

So reads mother from the Japanese bulletin board on the road-side. She smiles, looks at me and says simply, "We will go."

I sit beside mother. The newly built community hall
is spotless, smells fresh. There was a feeling of
great happiness in the air. Electricity was finally
installed several weeks ago in our camps
so that has increased the excitement.
Before, we had to bring battery microphones.
Now the new hall is brightly lit.

The seats are nearly all filled. We bring our own
cushions for the benches. Japanese lanterns are
again strung up along the stage. The favorite songs
of the people are blaring away from the gramophone.
Most of us know these old songs by heart,
so sing along with the singer.

Yuki sits at the back with Rose; I prefer to be
near the front. Mother beams; so does everyone.

They bow to one another and greet each other politely.
"Isn't this wonderful? " they whisper to one another.
"Yes, it's hard to believe we have electricity.
Now we don't have to walk to the main building to do
our ironing." "Thank God! I couldn't read at night.
My eyes. Now with proper light...."
"We must thank Goddess Quan-non."
An old man smiles happily at me, sucking his lower lip.

We hear the familiar starting sound of the Kabuki plays;
the hollow clop, clop, clop of two blocks of wood banged
together by a man dressed in a kimono. He kneels
before the drawn curtain as he does this. I love the sound.
Everyone becomes tense. Gossiping and laughing cease.
"Ahee begins our play..." he chants in an odd off-key
sing-song voice. I stare. The colored cherry-blossom-painted
curtain parts, and there we are in my parents' country....

Everyone claps, pleased. Then the musicians who
have silently seated themselves at the side of the stage
begin to chant. "They are explaining the story,"
mother whispers. "Watch." The string Japanese
banjo-like instrument twangs, two men kneeling beside
the musician close their eyes, are chanting;
their high voices are strange to my ears, and the language
they use is not the same as the one we speak at home.
It is an ancient language, sounds Indian.
My mouth opens. A heavily made-up man in black
samurai wig, white powder make-up, with red on
his forehead and around his glaring, fierce eyes,
comes slowly onto the stage. Some of his friends know him,
so shout, "Do your best! " His warrior armor looks stiff.
He stops, raises his white-stockinged left leg,
and turns to face the audience.
All his movements are slow and exaggerated.
Then he rolls his dark eyes, beneath the white

chalk make-up, says, "Eeeee! " shakes his head
from his shoulder, stamps his left leg down to the floor.
His right arm moves; he opens a moon-patterned fan,
then lifts his other leg, moves it about
and brings it down on the stage with a bang.
He starts to speak, rolls his eyes to the right and left,
then even crosses them. His painted red mouth goes down.
Another man shouts "Not bad. Keep it up! "
We shout encouragement to the players,
so it seems we become more part of it.
The samurai continues his dance. "Who's he? "
I whisper to mother. "He's a great warrior
and is going to a big battle soon.
The singers are saying this is his last battle,
so he is doing this to appease the gods
and for his wife and his mother."

Two women have appeared quietly to sit at the raised
platform. "Are they the ones? " I ask. "Yes! "
replies my mother. The two women are all made up also,
little thick eyebrows, pale face with red small lips.
They both have long-haired wigs which come down
to the floor. They both kneel, do not stir.
Then I see tears appear in the younger woman's eyes.
"....eeee...twang, twang..." goes the instrument.
The old man beside me blows his nose.
Mother's eyes are wet. "Great, keep it up! "
comes a voice from the back. Someone laughs,
breaks the tension. So slowly the old tale of how
a brave warrior went to battle is revealed....

At first, I watch. Then, as it progresses, because
the movements are so slow, and I do not
understand this ancient language, I fall asleep.
Mother nudges me, whispers, "Look, Shichan,
how it is." I open my eyes. "The warrior is dead.

They are bringing in his head! Watch! " I stare.
"It's in that round box; that's his enemy carrying it."
Everyone is quiet, the music has stopped.
The proud warrior all painted with blood on his armor
carries the head to his lords, kneels before them.

The silk-clad lord rises, seems to command him,
the kneeling one lifts the lid of the box. We all gasp.
A severed head with eyes closed is shown. I shudder,
poke mother and immediately close my eyes.
"That's terrible," I tell her.

I look at my round, white, bean cake the women's committee
has passed around. This is to celebrate the occasion.
I look at it, I love it, so I would like to save it. But,
"Aren't you going to eat it? " mother asks, smiles.
"Yes." I take a big bite. The lovely, dark, rose-sweet beans
in the center taste wonderful. I close my eyes....

We walk out of the building slowly.
Some blow their noses, because of the sad ending.
"My, the costumes were well done...."
"Imagine! They managed to bring the wigs from Vancouver."
They all talk, as we step out into the snow.
The light, yellow stars are twinkling.
Japanese music is playing again to send us all home.
It sounds cheerful. The white snow crunches
under our feet as we carefully make our way home.
This evening, for a time, war and our problems are
forgotten. There is a feeling in the crisp, cold air.

An incident

Summer is here once more. I often go for walks or pick berries
with Yuki and our friends. This morning I walk to the lake alone.

I walk happily through the woods. No one is in sight.
As I draw closer to the water, I hear a sound
I recognize. Buddhist prayer. I stop to listen.
It's Yoko-san, saying his morning prayers.

I look between the birch trees. There he is, waist deep,
in the quiet lake. His dark eyes are closed, his muscular
arms are raised, he is chanting. He looks weird
and out of place. I feel ill. I shudder and quietly turn
and head for home. I do not want him to see me.

I remember father saying to mother just the other day,
"I think he's harmless. I wouldn't worry too much,
there's no reason to report him." But I don't like
being near him. Neither does Yuki or Mrs. Kono.

Several days later a Mounted Police car draws up in front of
Yoko-san's house. Mr. Yoko is led by the policeman.
They get quietly into the car and drive away. No one comes
out of his house to say good-bye. That night father hears at the
bath-house that Mr. Yoko attacked the young girl, and she has
just given birth to a child right in the house. We are so
surprised for she did not look pregnant.

A month later, I see the girl again. She sits silently in front of
the house. She does not see us any more. Her eyes are dead
behind her round glasses. She just sits there and ignores the
baby. Her mother tends it as if it were her own. I see the
baby all wrapped up and I feel sad. The girl seems so alone.
I wonder how she feels. Every time I walk by her house, I think
about her. Her brothers seem more unto themselves than ever.
We see them less and less, as if they are slowly disappearing.

Winter 1944
Fire

Another spring and summer have gone by. Nothing special
happens, just the usual quarrels and complaints about our
conditions, war, and so on. Then, one day, early in the winter
evening....

We are sitting by the stove.
The hollow sound of the metal bell rings, "clang...clang...."
Mother says, "That's the fire bell! "
We stop talking, listen. Father looks up from
under his metal reading glasses, "You're right! "
He springs to his feet, puts on his boots and coat
and rushes out of our house into the snow.
He shouts, "It's coming from road 'R' area."
I hear him running. There are shouts outside,
as others hear the fire bell. "Clang...clang...clang...."
It continues to ring. Mr. Kono soon runs after father.
We too run out. "A bucket brigade is needed! "
Someone is shouting, "Fire...fire...in road 'R'...hurry...."

I see the orange, red tongues of flame in the dark night.
Mother, Yuki and I go closer. We think it's Mary's house.
I feel terrible, then relieved as I see it's Mr. Sakura's
house next to hers.

The living flame is strangely beautiful in the
dark, starless night. Its orangy, moving fire dances
against the deep, blue sky. Crackling sparks fly
in different directions. I stop and stare.
It eats the tiny wooden house with mad joy.
The men, my father, Mr. Kono, everyone is helping.
They form a bucket brigade. But it is not enough.
They look like little ants trying to douse water
on a big fiery dragon. The frail house totters,

collapses like a burnt matchbox. There is no wind,
so the fire does not spread. Fortunate, for all the houses
are built quite close together and the trees are all around them.
If this had happened in the summer....

I do not stay until the end. I go home.
As I enter, I turn to see the flames still leaping
up into the night. The hungry, empty air draws the
flame and feeds it. The whole camp is out. The gong
high up on the pole is still being beaten by someone.
It creates a horrible tension in the night.
Fear is in the night. I hurry inside and go to bed,
hide my head under the blanket....

Next morning on the way to school,
we see the burnt remains of the house.
It is charred, black ashes. Only the black, burnt beams
remain. We are told about the couple who lived there.
Mr. Sakura was hurt. The clothes he was drying by
the stove caught fire while he was asleep. Mrs. Sakura
was visiting a friend. Apparently, he woke up
in time, rushed out of his house, then remembered
his money-box and ran back into the burning house.
He did not find it. They say he had to be pulled out
— he was burnt and taken to the hospital in New Denver.

I stand and stare at the sooty ruins.
Mary says, "I was scared. I thought our house was
going to go too. I saw you standing there with
your mother for awhile. You left early? "
"Yes. I'm glad it wasn't your house, Mary.
I don't like fires. They bother me. I went to bed."

We stare. "It's like a dream, isn't it, Mary?
Yesterday, the house was here. Now it's gone."
I feel strange. Nothing is permanent.

Some women return to stare too, the gossipmongers,
they chuckle, sigh, click their loose false teeth.
They breathe hard in the cold. "Ahee," they say.
"Sakura-san has been drinking again, sins of liquor.
I wonder how much money he lost."
Mr. Shimizu appears, steps into the ruins, sifts around.
The air is still and very heavy. The strong smell
of the burnt wood, clothes, remains in the air.
Mary and I back away, continue on to school.
We are silent. The melting snow sounds funny
under our feet. I look up at the pale, blue sky.
I wonder about God. What causes tragedy?
Mother always says, "It's karma. He must have done
something to earn it." I do not quite understand.
The Japanese always say this, "Karma, karma."
Yuki says mother is a bit superstitious.
I wonder. I feel there is something more to it.

The whole community takes part in a collection to give money
and clothes to Mr. Sakura and his family. The other camps from
outlying areas send money, too. So they are able to start over
again. A new house is given them. Soon the fire is no longer
talked about. Only the charred remains of the house are there
to remind us each time we pass Mary's....

10

The last year
March 1945

I am in my last year in school, grade eight. We read in the papers
that the Axis countries are now losing the war. The people in
the camp quarrel about the future.

May
Germany surrenders

There is silence in our camp. Some seem relieved; others, confused. Father insists on returning to Japan. He is still very
bitter about the way the Canadian Government has treated us.
David has written us not to sign to return. He says the
people in Ontario were curious and suspicious at first, but it's
changed.

"Jobs we could not hold in Vancouver are open
to us here," he writes. "Many have been kind
and helped us. If you insist upon returning to Japan,
I want you to know that I will not join you,
but will remain in Canada." Yuki says, "See.
There *is* a future for us here." Mother looks at father,
"I will not go back to Japan without my children."
She tries to make it sound gentle; she speaks very quietly,
but father stiffens. His hands clench; his lips tighten.
I am so confused. Why do we have to make such
decisions?

Yuki has finished high school. She has been able to get a job as
a typist with the British Columbia Security Commission. I am
happy for her. The office is not far from us; it's in a house like
ours which has been converted.

Yuki tells me about her job. "Dad is always in there,
in our office to complain. You should hear the way he

and Mr. Sumi talk to Mr. Baldwin. Mr. Baldwin is nice to us, but he sure doesn't like dad. He's so blunt."

Father and Mr. Sumi are trying to get higher wages for the men, for they have to pay for the electricity. Even the Government seems confused about our future....No one seems to know what to do with us. Bit by bit, the regulations of how we must live become more relaxed. Now, we are allowed to have a radio, though not a short wave one. David kindly sends us a small, brown radio. This is lovely. We hear popular music for the first time since we left Vancouver over two years ago. We are the only ones in the camp who have such a treasure. All our friends come, especially on Saturday nights to hear the hit-parade and other programs. We cheer and scream with other teenagers when Frank Sinatra sings our favorite songs. The tiny box has brought the outside world closer to us. We hear the news directly. Father listens to the news, he often frowns, looks worried. He does not speak much. He is worried about his family in Japan, for now Tokyo and the mainland are being bombed and that is where his brothers and sisters live.

June

David writes to Yuki to move to Toronto if she can, for now a few people are allowed to leave for the east, provided they have a close relative to look after them. Mother tells her quietly to go. Father is not told. Mother says, "Better that he does not know." So we all keep silent.

July

Yuki's papers come through. Working in the office with Mr. Baldwin helps. Soon, the date is set, father is told. He is very upset and hurt, but accepts it. Some of his friends, however, take it badly.

Mr. and Mrs. Shimizu come all the way from
another camp, thirty miles away.
He is a tiny man, has many children,
all in camp with him for they are young.
He narrows his eyes and asks Yuki, "Why do you want
to go to Toronto? You like to be called a 'Jap'?
Be a third-class citizen? Do you think you can ever vote?
You're Japanese! Return to Japan, to your motherland!
That is your duty!" Yuki replies,
"I don't want to go to Japan." Father looks angry,
shouts, "Shut up, Yuki, you're my daughter.
You are Japanese." Mr. Shimizu steps back,
startled. His eyes narrow, "You are a traitor! Do you hear?"
Mrs. Shimizu stands up from the table, comes forward,
quietly speaks, puts out her hand to Yuki.
"We are all returning to Japan. We are taking
all the children. Come with us. Start a new life!"
Yuki is angry now. "But can't you understand?
Japan will lose the war. The whole country is being
bombed every day. *They won't want us back there.*"
She is half-crying, half-shouting now.

I join in. "That's right. They just bombed Tokyo again!"
Father turns on me. "Be quiet, Shichan.
You don't know anything. If I return to Japan,
you'll come with me!" I start to cry.
Mr. Shimizu says, "Why are you crying?
There's nothing to cry about."
Yuki runs out of the house. I follow. I feel terrible,
I want to go to Toronto with Yuki, but I am too young,
so I just sit and cry....

So it is that our family is further divided. Yuki leaves for
Toronto. Father does not say good-bye to her. Mother looks
very sad. I feel terrible too. Mother says she prays each day
that she will not see her family separated.

A walk with Mary

Mary and I go for a walk in the woods.
We sit on a stump, we listen, hear the chirping of the birds.
Insects make a wild racket as they sun themselves.
All around us, everything is green, the moss under our feet,
the maple trees, the ferns. All in different shades of green.
How lovely it all is! I feel at peace.

"What if your father really decides to go to Japan,
Shichan? " Mary asks. I am looking at the blue sky,
hidden a little by the trees. I look down,
remember our problems. They seemed so far away
at that moment. "Mother says she and I will go east.
David and Yuki will look after us. She says
she's sure father won't leave us,
then she goes and prays that he won't."

Mary says, "At first my parents wanted to go to Japan, too.
Now they don't know what to do. Dad's still very bitter
about losing everything. He worked hard all his life.
Now he has to start all over, here or in Japan.
My brothers in Toronto want us to come and join them.
But you know, I think my parents are scared."

I look at Mary. She is thirteen now,
We are both getting older and beginning
to understand lots of things. Mary looks older than her age.
I have known her since we came to camp. I wonder
if we'll be friends after we move to the big city. I hope so.

"My father is still furious about Yuki," I tell her,
"because we didn't tell him when Yuki got
her papers to move to Toronto. He hides it,
but I know he's angry. Mother says some of
his friends aren't speaking to him for allowing it.

Can you believe it? Some adults are so
narrowminded and prejudiced."

I look at Mary and smile. We are friends.
Strange to think that to some people we are
only "orientals," and that they really hate us.
I move my feet. The moss feels soft under
my running-shoes. I listen to the birds....

August 1945

We hear the terrifying news. The atomic bomb! Father and
mother are silent. Mrs. Kono looks so upset. I go to see Mary.
Her mother is crying. There is a terrible tension in the camp.
Mr. Mori and the other veterans are openly cursed and threat-
ened. Some blame them for the bomb. No one speaks to
Mr. Mori. I saw him this morning. He stared at me. He held
his stick very tight to his thin body. I backed away and turned,
for I didn't want to pass him. I wondered what he thought as I
hurried into the house. I can't understand all this hatred,
especially among ourselves....

The end of the war

At last the war with Japan is at an end! We are not surprised,
we have been expecting it for months now. It hits the older
people very hard. They are given two choices by the Canadian
Government: to sign a paper and renounce their Canadian
citizenship and return to Japan, or to remain here and be re-
located elsewhere. There are terrible quarrels. Those who have
signed to return to Japan are called "fools"; the ones who have
chosen to stay in Canada are called "dogs", slang for traitors. The
Kono family, Mr. Shimizu, our father's friend, all sign to return
to Japan. We feel sad that Kay-ko is leaving us. All those families
must move to another camp, at Tashme, not far from Vancouver.
From there, they will go to Vancouver, then on to Japan.

My mother and I just wait, hoping. Then one day,
out of the blue, father says quietly: "We go east!
I've placed an application. We sign to go to Toronto."
He speaks quietly, more to mother than to me.
"It is useless to return now. My family, God knows
where they are, if any are still alive. I'm glad it's over.
We'll just have to start again. It won't be easy for us."
He looks strange. He rises from his chair quickly
and walks out. I feel sorry for him. The atomic bomb
has upset everyone deeply, too. It seems so wrong.
Mother looks at me, smiles. Her eyes beam.
"See, I told you, I told you, he would see the sense
in remaining here. We can't return to Japan.
They have nothing now, no food, clothes,
houses for their own people. Here, we have each other.
Write to Yuki and David." I write immediately.

Yuki is in Hamilton, Ontario, living with another friend. I am
so happy, so is mother. Father is quiet, but he starts to make
boxes with our cousin, Mr. Fujiwara, the carpenter, to pack our
clothes in. Our cousins are remaining in camps awhile longer,
but they, too, have signed to stay in Canada.

Mother and I begin to pack. I have to leave many things
I have grown to love behind. My favorite "dutch shoe"
which Yuki gave me almost two Christmases ago
is still by my bed, on the narrow shelf near the candle.
I pick it up. The candies and nuts are gone.
The sparkly, gold rice is dull,
many grains have already fallen off;
more drop into my hand. But as I hold it
I can still feel the love which the kind Sisters
put into it just when we needed love so much.
I place it back on the shelf. It is too fragile to pack.

September 1945

It is almost three years to the day since we left Vancouver. The
papers for us to leave for the east come through. This is our last
week in New Denver.

I go to the lake for the last time with mother
to rinse our clothes. The water is still warm.
I swish the white sheets in the clear water.
Mother is wringing the clothes. She is singing,
she looks so happy. I wonder what David will
look like. I say, "We won't be doing this in Toronto."
Mother sighs, stops, looks at the mountains.
"All in all, Shichan, the three years have not been very hard,
when you think of all the poor people who have been
killed and hurt, and now the suffering in Japan."

Mother and I look out into the distance. A small bird
swoops gracefully down towards the still water.
Another follows. Their pure joy in doing this
is reflected in their flight. The morning mist is slowly
rising from the lake. It looks like it is on fire.
The sun's rays try to seep through the mist.
Everything looks all misty and gray-yellow. I know
I shall remember this beautiful scene,
doing our chores for the last time with nature
all-giving and so silent. Mother bends her frail body,
continues to rinse the clothes. I go back to helping her.
There is warmth between us, and I feel her happiness.

I try to absorb it all, for I know it will be gone soon.
Toronto is a large city. David has written
it is in flat country, by Lake Ontario.
There are no mountains, no snow-capped mountains.
Instead will be concrete buildings, apartments, buses, cars.
But I am looking forward to this, too. Instead of

the sounds of insects and frogs and wild dogs at night,
we will have street sounds, and go to school with
other children, all kinds of children.

Our last night in camp, I go out of the house.
I watch the red rays of the glorious sun.
It spreads its burning arms to the brilliant early autumn
sky, touches the dark pines in the distance.
They catch fire. I hold my breath.
It is aflame, all red for a long time.

Then the rays of the sun slowly begin to fade
behind the now deep purple mountains. The trees,
the mountains all turn into a dark mysterious silhouette as
I stay rooted to the spot. Night comes on.
The pale, pale moon is suspended in the scarlet sky.
I stay standing a long time watching it,
for I want to remember it forever.

Epilogue

Toronto, Ontario

June 7, 1964

Nineteen years have passed. Tonight I have come here to watch the end of a story. I am standing before a gray concrete, fortresslike building with a crowd of my people, all Japanese-Canadians. They have come from all over Ontario to be at this outdoor ceremony. After years of planning and money-raising, the Japanese Canadian Cultural Centre is ready.

It is early evening. The late spring sun casts a warm ochre glow over everything. I stand towards the back of the crowd. The older people are seated at the front, but father and mother are not there. "I don't want to go," father said earlier when I asked him. The years have lined his face and tinged his spiky black hair with gray, but they have not softened his intensity. I looked at mother. Her gold-rimmed glasses flashed. "I'll stay home with your father tonight."

But many others are here. Yuki, with her husband and three children. Patty, the youngest, comes to stand beside me, takes my hand. "Mommy's wearing a new hat." I laugh, we all laugh and Yuki makes a face at Patty. Yuki is still very close to me. After all these years our love for each other has not changed. I see David in the distance with his wife and four children. They look like tiny theater dolls, with their dark hair, snappy round eyes, all dressed up. Patty calls to them. They wave back and jump up and down. Further on, I see the Kono family. After moving to Tashme on the coast, at the last minute — like many other families — they changed their minds and asked permission to remain in Canada. They had difficult years working in northern Ontario and had

94

finally moved to Toronto. They are still our friends. Kay-ko
is married now, but her round, beautiful eyes are still the
same. I continue to search the crowd. Our cousins, the
Fujiwaras, are away down front with the older people.

Suddenly, a hush falls over the crowd. A shiny black limousine
pulls up. Everyone turns, watching it. A group of officials
have been waiting for it. They move forward as the door
is opened. Out of it gets a smiling man and woman: the
Prime Minister of Canada, Lester B. Pearson, and
Mrs. Pearson. We watch them go towards the platform.

As the speeches start, my mind wanders back, tracing the years.

We are moved east from the camp, only to find that the
quota of Japanese permitted to live in Toronto is filled, and
there are no jobs. My parents go to work as domestic servants
for an American family in Oakville, father to do the gardening
and cooking and mother to clean and care for their small
child. I cannot join them, father tells me gently, for the estate
is in the country and there are no schools nearby. He talks it
over with mother and David, and I am to go to Hamilton to
stay with Yuki. David will send the money for me to continue
school.

The Oakville family is very kind — not all of our friends are
so lucky — and we are allowed to come and see our parents.
At Christmas, the family leaves for a holiday in Mexico and
all of us, Yuki, David and I, come for the holidays. Mother
looks so happy and father cooks and outdoes himself. We seem
to feast and rejoice for days.

At high school in Hamilton I take art as my major subject.
The next summer, I get a job as summer help to a family
with three children. I like the children but not their mother
who makes what were to be "light duties" very heavy, and

had somewhere got the idea that Japanese don't like to eat.
In the fall of 1946, David helps us to buy a house in Toronto
and we can all be together again. Father finds work in
Toronto as a gardener and part-time cook for another
wealthy family. They are so kind and generous that father
stays there until he retires fourteen years later.

I finish high school, go on to the Ontario College of Art.
At graduation, father and mother make me a gift from the
savings they have gathered so slowly through the years so
that I can go to Europe to continue my studies. Yuki marries,
David marries, and a new generation starts, unclouded by
those things that happened to their parents so long ago....

I focus back on the voices from the platform. The Prime
Minister is introduced. He talks of all the fine things
Japanese-Canadians have done for Canada; I feel a nervous
tension go through the crowd as he comes to the hardships
we suffered during World War II:

*"...The action of the Canadian Government of the day
— though taken under the strains and fears and pressures
and irrationalities of war — was a black mark against
Canada's traditional fairness and devotion to the principles
of human rights. We have no reason to be proud of this
episode nor are we...."*

I look at the faces near me and feel the private silence of each
listener. Some stare at their laps; others have their eyes closed.
Some stare out at the sky, eyes moist. I look up too, and see
the vast orange sky.... I remember how often I stood outside
our house in the New Denver camp and watched the sun set. The
sun, the sky look the same, still beautiful, patient, so knowing....

Afterwards I go back to my parents' house. Mother brings
green tea. Father is drinking beer. Mother sits beside him.

96

They are inseparable now. Mother looks at me and smiles.
Her small face is imprinted with the hardship of the years,
her silvery hair is grown thin, but her eyes behind her round
glasses are the same, warm.

Mother and I sip tea. The room is still. I say,
"The Prime Minister said that what Canada did was wrong.
Did you hear?" Father replies stiffly, "Yes, I heard it on
the radio." Mother and I look at him and wait. He takes a
drink of beer from his glass, puts it down, stares at it. Then
with gusto he takes another, longer drink that drains the glass.
At last he speaks, looking straight ahead of him. "I'm glad
the Prime Minister said that."

Mother nods and nudges him. They both look at me.
I feel their happiness come toward me, and I smile back.

An afterword

This story is based on what actually happened to me and other people of Japanese origin living in Canada. Names of individuals and certain incidents have been altered in some cases to give anonymity to those involved (not all of us care to be reminded or questioned about those painful years); in other cases, to keep the account simple.

Nineteen years passed following World War II before that night in 1964 when Prime Minister Lester Pearson admitted the "black mark" against Canada that the internment of Canadians of Japanese origin represented. It would take another twenty-four years before another Prime Minister, Brian Mulroney, speaking officially in the House of Commons condemned the internment and offered financial redress.

The compensation was long, long overdue. Of the 22,000 unjustly interned, only 12,000 were alive to be "compensated."

At war's end, almost 4,000 of us were expelled from Canada or chose to go to war-ravaged Japan rather than remain in the uncertain hostile climate here. Their citizenship was revoked.

The National Association of Japanese Canadians carried on the long negotiations and the compensation arrangement was hard-won. It will give each survivor individual payment of $21,000. Those whose citizenship was revoked will have it restored. Twelve million dollars will be set aside to promote educational, social and cultural activities that contribute to the well-being of the community or that will promote human rights. Twenty-four million dollars will be used to create a Canadian Race Relations Foundation that will foster racial harmony and cross-cultural understanding and help eliminate racism. One half of this endowment will be recognized as a commemoration of those who suffered injustice.

My parents and most of their generation are gone. It is for us to remember and never allow such injustice to occur again.

Shizuye "Shichan" Takashima,
Toronto, Canada 1989

A Personal Note

I was really two years older than I picture myself; I felt younger than my actual years, perhaps because I felt so helpless. Yuki, my sister, remains as she was. I have four brothers, not one. ''David'' is a composite I used to keep the account uncomplicated. All four of my brothers were moved east to camps and subjected to the identical experience. In 1944, Joseph, the youngest, joined the Canadian Army and was stationed in India. Many Japanese-Canadians did the same, including Yuki's husband-to-be who was with my brother in India.

My thanks to my family for their interest in my endeavors.

S.T.

Artist Takashima was eleven years old during World War II when she and her family along with 22,000 other Canadians of Japanese origin were removed from their homes on the west coast of Canada and sent to internment camps in the interior. She would spend the next three years there and the memory of that bewildering time remained so real to her that thirty years later she could reproduce it in words and paintings of remarkable vividness.

Her childhood had been difficult even before the internment. A premature birth had left her unusually small of stature and with a slight limp. The worries her parents shared with all the other uprooted families were intensified by their concern for her. The internment was in the Canadian Rockies where fathers were sent ahead to build shacks for the families. The magnificent scenery became an ironic background to the hardships and indignities and played an important role in her development as an artist.

The internment has often been called the most disgracefully racist episode in Canadian history since no person of Japanese origin was ever accused of disloyalty. Racism against immigrants from Asia existed from their first arrival on the west coast; the war with Japan added hysteria and provided the excuse for the relocation and seizure of property. At war's end, that racism further expressed itself in the government's efforts to get the internees to renounce their Canadian citizenship and return to Japan.